so easy...
Beading
learn to bead with 25 great projects

Liz Thornton & Jean Power

St Martin's Griffin
New York

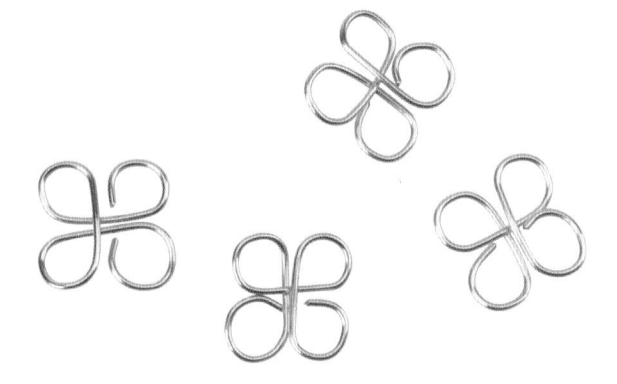

Illustrations and compilation by Carroll & Brown Limited 2006
Managing Art Editor Emily Cook
Photography Roger Dixon

Library of Congress Cataloging-in-Publication Data Available Upon Request

ISBN 0-312-35924-1
ISBN-13 978-0-312-35924-9

First published in the United Kingdom by Carroll & Brown Publishers Limited

First U.S. Edition: September 2006

10 9 8 7 6 5 4 3 2 1

Reproduced in Singapore by Colourscan
Printed in China

Contents

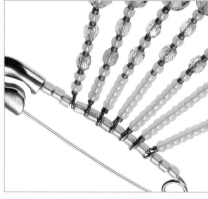

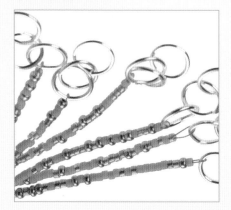
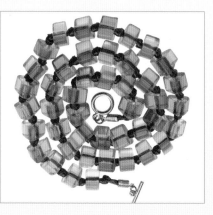

Introduction

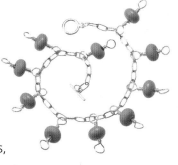

You'll be surprised by just how easy it is to get started making your own unique beading projects, from bracelets, earrings and necklaces to more exotic creations. With a few basic tools and materials and some carefully chosen beads, you can let your imagination run riot.

There are so many outlets selling beading materials now that you will be spoiled for choice. And if there's something you can't find in the stores, the number of beading websites is incredible – and growing – so it's unlikely that you won't be able to find something that appeals, whatever your taste.

This book begins with the basics – finding the right beads, threading materials, findings and tools, planning a design and using crimps. By this time you'll want to get on with your beading, so we have included some simple to make but stunning projects to get you started. Right from the beginning – and throughout the book – you will find the core techniques you will need to master to give your creations that professional look.

One of the best things about beading – apart from the beads themselves – is the number of looks and effects you can achieve. Different threading materials, such as leather thong, fabric cords, different thicknesses and colors of beading wire, can all make a great difference to the finished look of your chosen beads. Apart from using other, smaller, beads to maximize your "showcase" beads, you can make the most of more expensive beads by knotting fabrics and using wrapped wires. By learning how to work with wire you can create a huge range of looks, from simple "floating" necklaces to fabulous bracelets and belts.

Of course, once you master the techniques we have included you can begin to plan and design your own creations, but we hope that you will get as much pleasure from the projects we have included as we did designing them.

Liz Thornton & Jean Power

Finding the right beads

Beads have one thing in common – a hole through which they can be threaded! They are made of many different materials and come in lots of shapes and sizes – way too many for us to use more than a tiny selection for the projects in this book. We chose beads from as wide a range of materials as we could and which we think you will find readily in your local craft or bead store.

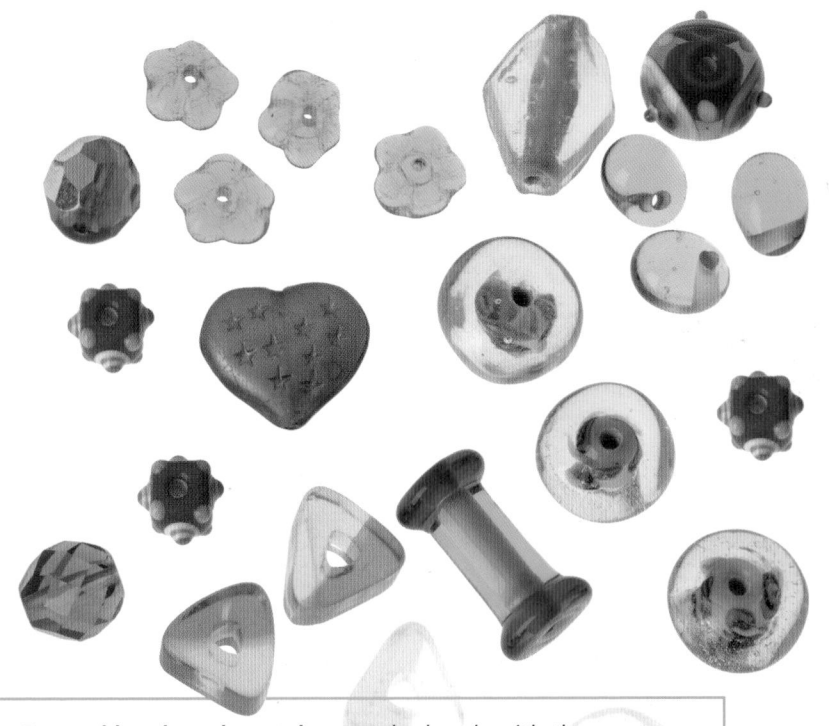

GLASS BEADS

Beads made of glass are the most commonly sold. They vary enormously in size, ranging from tiny seed beads to handmade lampwork beads nearly an inch across. Glass beads can be surprisingly heavy and they are, of course, breakable. The beads we have used are:

Seed beads – small round beads, generally available in sizes 8 and 11, though they come both smaller and larger in specialist stores. "Pony" beads are just about the largest of this type, and they are commonly available in craft stores (pony beads are also made in plastic). Seed beads are useful for filling in spaces between larger beads to help show them off to best effect.

Cylinder beads – tube-shaped beads with straight sides. They come in two sizes, standard and double. Delica is the brand of cylinder bead we have used, though there are others available.

Faceted beads and crystals – are the beads with the most sparkle! The surface of the bead has been cut and polished to give many sides that reflect the light. Beads made of crystal have a higher lead content than plain glass, giving even greater brilliance, though at a higher cost. These beads are usually described by their shape (eg bi-cone or square) and diameter in millimeters.

Lampwork beads – are made in a flame from glass rods. Each one is individually made so they can be quite special (and, of course, expensive).

Other glass beads – we have used various sizes of larger round beads and some other shapes, too, such as drops and cubes, flowers, tear drops, fruit shapes, ovals, leaves, rondelles and even dumbbells. Some of these are pressed glass beads that have been made in moulds – look carefully and you might see the "seam" running around the center where the two halves of the mould met.

SHELLS AND BONE BEADS

Small shells come in their original shape, while larger shells are more usually cut into smaller pieces. A hole is drilled through the shell for threading. Some shells are their natural color while some are dyed. Even the largest shell beads, however, are light and therefore easy to wear. The same is true of beads made from bone or horn – they are light for their size. Bone beads are often carved.

STONE BEADS

Stone beads are cut and polished into many different shapes – we have used flat and large ovals, chunks and chips. Semi-precious stones – rose quartz, for example – are more economical than gem stones such as amethyst. You can expect all stone beads to be heavy for their size, but they have surprisingly small holes.

METAL BEADS

Metal beads are generally hollow and made from thin sheets of metal. Silver or gold finishes, sometimes "antiqued", are the most commonly available. They can also have a surface finish added, such as enamel, for example.

PLASTIC BEADS

Plastic beads are light and colorful, though often without the shine of a glass bead. Being cheaper and less fragile than glass, plastic beads could be substituted for many of the beads we have used in the book, and are especially good for youngsters. Sequins are very thin plastic discs – usually flat – but some of those we used are cupped into a flower shape.

CERAMIC BEADS

Ceramic beads can be bought in many different styles, from plain and undecorated to exquisite Chinese painted designs. Often, painted ceramic beads are glazed to protect their surface designs. The ceramic beads we used are terracotta with a pattern painted on the surface.

Threading materials

Each of the materials we have used to thread our beads has its own particular use, as you will see in the projects later in the book. Take care to choose a threading material that will fit your chosen beads, especially if you need to go through the hole more than once.

FLEXIBLE BEADING WIRE

This type of wire (sometimes called "bead stringing wire" or "cable") is very strong and is made of several strands of stainless steel twisted together inside a nylon coating. It is manufactured in several thicknesses, strengths and colors, and the number of strands twisted together to make the final wire also varies. All this information should be given on the spool, so you can check carefully that you are buying the right wire. Generally speaking, those with a high number of fine strands are more flexible (and more expensive) than those with fewer but thicker strands. One problem associated with these wires is a tendency to kink if bent too sharply. And, once kinked, they will stay that way! So take care to handle and store your jewelry carefully.

LEATHER CORD

Leather cord or thong is a favorite for beaders, being attractive, economical and easy to use. There is no fraying when the cord is cut, so no need to treat the ends. Leather cords are available in a wide range of colors, giving lots of scope for making interesting designs. They also come in different thicknesses, so you can choose the one that will suit your beads best.

SATIN CORD

Satin cords (often called "rattail") are lovely, shiny cords that come in a beautiful array of colors. It is important to treat the ends when you cut them as they might fray (see page 37).

EMBROIDERY THREAD

Threads intended for embroidery are very useful to the beader. They come in a huge range of colors and finishes. Because they are generally quite light and fine, you will find them most useful if you use several thicknesses together. Some people find that a bit fiddly, but it gives you the added advantage of being able to mix your thread colors to blend even better with your beads – all those choices! Embroidery threads are not manufactured for their strength, however, so you cannot expect them to bear the heaviest beads or to wear for as long as some of the more heavyweight cords.

ELASTIC CORD

Stretchy cord made of elastic gives a really quick result for a bracelet or necklace and, because there's no need for a clasp, the results are easy to wear. The cord comes in a range of several colors and in varying thicknesses. The two most commonly found are 1 mm and 0.5 mm in diameter. Make sure to use the thickest cord your beads will accommodate – the thicker the cord, the stronger it is. Any elastic cord will break, however, if stretched too far!

METAL WIRE

Metal wire is strong and hardwearing. We generally use silver-plated or gold-plated wires as they are firm and hold their shape well once bent. The softer craft wires tend to be rather flimsy which makes them more difficult to use effectively. That said, they come in a fabulous range of colors that can be very difficult to resist! Wires are available in different thicknesses. The diameter of wires manufactured in the US is given by gauge number (the higher the number, the finer the wire); the diameter of wires manufactured elsewhere is given in millimeters.

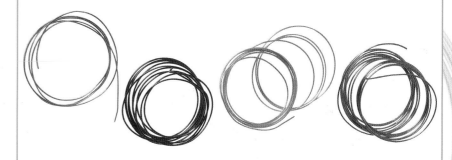

HEMP

Look in the macramé section of your craft store and you will be likely to find colored hemp cords. They are great for knotting and stringing beads, being very strong and reasonably priced. They can be a little rough, however, and will give a stiffer result than the finer, softer embroidery threads.

Useful findings

Findings are those small items, usually metal, which help you to finish a piece of jewelry.

Available in many designs, sizes, and metals, the choice of which one to use is up to you.

Whilst these may seem like insignificant items, choosing and using the right finding can have

a big effect on the practicality of your finished item as well as its look.

WATCH FACE

Many bead stores sell watch faces separately for you to add your own band to, or you can use a watch you already own. The only thing to bear in mind is how the watchband will be attached. Some watches have a loop you can thread through, others have a bar that may not suit the look of your finished piece.

CRIMPS

Crimps are small metal beads designed to be squashed – or crimped – to help finish your work. Available in two main shapes, round or tubular, they are both used in the same way. Your flexible wire is threaded through a crimp, a clasp, and then back through the crimp, and squashed with a pair of flat or crimping pliers. The crimp then bites into the nylon coating of the wire and holds it tight. When buying your flexible wire check which size crimp it needs, as using the incorrect crimp will result in it breaking. See pages 16–17 for more details on crimping.

CLASPS

Used to fasten your jewelry, clasps come in many different styles and sizes. Some examples are a toggle or t-bar clasp, a lobster fastening, an s-hook or a bolt ring. When choosing your clasp bear in mind ease of use. For example, a bracelet will be fastened single-handed, so a toggle clasp is a better choice than a screw barrel.

SIEVE

These metal disks are used to make many different finished items such as brooches, earrings, tiepins, and button covers. The top disk has lots of holes through which you can thread your wire, beads, sequins etc. After you have added your beadwork and decorated it as much as you want, place the two disks together and fold down the tabs to hold them securely in place.

JUMP RINGS

These are metal rings that are commonly used to attach findings and clasps to each other. However, you can also use them to make your own chains, or mix them with beads to make jewelry. See pages 26–7 for more details on jump rings.

EARRING FINDINGS

There are many styles of finding to link your beadwork to your ear, the most common being a hook-shaped wire. For more details on planning earrings see pages 28–9.

SPLIT RINGS

Similar to jump rings, split rings will be most familiar to you as used on key-rings. They are more secure than jump rings, because of the way the metal loops around, but they are also more tricky to open. They can be used for attaching findings, or as one end of a clasp that can be hooked into.

END BARS

Similar to spacer bars, end bars are designed to sit at the ends of your strands of beads, separating them and making a bridge between the beadwork and clasp. Some will come with an integral clasp others will need a clasp added. See page 33 for more information on using end bars.

KEY-RINGS

These can be decorated with wire and beadwork to be used as key-rings or as bag charms. Different types and sizes are available and some may come with chain already attached for you to decorate.

HEAD PINS AND EYE PINS

These lengths of metal wire are just the thing for adding beads and dangles to your jewelry. Eye pins have a small loop of metal at one end; head pins have either a flat or decorative end. Both come in different metals, thicknesses, and lengths, and some can be easier to bend than others.

CORD CRIMPS

Cord crimps attach the cord to a clasp. Whether you're using leather, hemp, fabric, or other cord, simply place the end into the crimp and squeeze it shut to trap the cord. Some cord crimps come with an integral clasp, for others you may have to attach a clasp. See page 37 for more information on using cord crimps.

END CONES

These are designed to be both decorative and useful. End cones hide the join between multiple strands of beads and the clasp. Available in many styles, sizes, and metals, choose one that complements your beads and maybe even matches your clasp. See page 82 for more information on using end cones.

SPACER BARS

These decorative findings also have a functional purpose. Designed to separate your strands in a multi-strand piece so that it lies as you intended, these bars come in different sizes and can be very plain, so as not to stand out, or decorative to enhance your finished piece. See page 33 for more information on using spacer bars.

SAFETY PINS

Safety pins are a great way of making quick decorative jewelry. Many bead stores now sell colored pins just for this purpose. You can also get safety pins on which the head screws off so you can add dangles to one side while the other side pins through your clothes or bag.

CHAIN

Purchased chain can be easily decorated with bead dangles – and with the addition of a clasp, you'll soon have a finished piece of jewelry. Available in different metals and styles, ready-made chain is a great item to have in your materials box if you don't want to spend time on making your own.

Tools

One of the first rules when using tools is always to think about safety. Some tools have blades or cutters, or even close spaces where your fingers might get trapped or pinched. Also, bear in mind that if you're cutting wire, the piece you're cutting might fly off and hit you – or someone else. On the other hand, trying to cut wire with a blunt cutter is no fun and can be dangerous! Always try to buy the best quality tools you can. Good tools will last you a long time and will help you to create better, more professionally finished jewelry.

SCISSORS

Make sure your scissors are sharp, as this will give you a neat, accurate cut that will result in a better finish. Never use your scissors for cutting wire!

WIRE CUTTERS

These are available in different styles (such as side cutters, flush cutters, semi-flush cutters, and nibblers). Any of these are fine for making jewelry and will give you the result you want. See page 58–9 for more details on cutting wire.

PLIERS

When choosing pliers try to ensure that they are made for jewelry making and are therefore lighter, easier to use, and have smooth inner jaws that won't bite into your metal. Pliers can come in different sizes, with different size jaws for bolder or more delicate work. The pliers listed below are the main ones you will need for most jewelry making.

Snipe or chain nose pliers *These are similar to flat nose pliers, however their jaws taper to a point toward the end. This means you can use them to get into tighter spaces or to form smaller bends. They can also be used to squash crimp beads.*

Flat nose pliers *These pliers have flat jaws that are the same width along the whole length. Useful for holding findings or wire as you work, these are also used to make bends and wrap loops and for squashing crimps. See pages 16–17 for more information on crimping.*

Crimping pliers *These pliers are essential if you plan to do a lot of stringing and crimping. Specially made for crimping, they have two separate notches that you use first to squeeze your crimp and then to fold it over to give a rounder, more professional look to your work.*

Round nose pliers *Used mainly for making loops, these pliers have rounded jaws that taper to a point toward the end. When making loops, always try to form the loop on the same section of the pliers' jaws, so that your loops all finish the same size. You can make a mark on the jaws with a permanent marker or some masking tape to help you use the same point each time.*

BEAD OR JEWELRY BOARD

A bead board or jewelry board can be very useful in helping you plan and bead your finished design. These boards have grooves on them with measurements alongside so that you can place your beads to work out your final length. They also come with divided sections to hold your beads while you plan and work. See pages 14–15 for more details on planning your designs.

BEAD MAT

A piece of fabric or a beading mat that you lay on top of your working surface is essential to stop your beads rolling around. You can buy beading mats from most bead stores or use a piece of fabric you already have – velvet is a good choice.

PIN BOARD AND THUMB TACKS

Particularly useful when knotting (when you may find you don't have enough hands to hold your work and knot at the same time), you may find it useful to pin your work onto a surface to hold it still while you work. You can purchase a pin board that will take thumb tacks and not damage your working surface. You can also use a macramé board, if you have one, a cork tile, or a bulletin board. See pages 38–9 and 44–5 for more information on tying knots.

NEEDLE OR AWL FOR KNOTS

When tying knots it can sometimes be hard to position your knot before it tightens. Use an awl or large, blunt needle that you place in the knot, so when you slide it toward your bead it won't tighten. Once you're happy with the positioning, remove the awl and pull the knot tight. See pages 38–9 and 44–5 for more information on tying knots.

FILES

When working with wire you may need to file the ends to remove any sharp edges. You can purchase specially made metal jewelry files or use files you already own – or even emery boards. See pages 58–9 for more information on cutting and filing wire.

RULER OR MEASURING TAPE

If you want your finished piece of jewelry to fit well, accuracy is important from the start. Using a measuring tape or ruler to check your measurements, rather than estimating, will help you to achieve a great result. See pages 14–15 for more information on planning your designs.

Planning a design

Before you start to string any piece of jewelry it is always worth spending some time thinking about your design. There are some things you'll need to take into account – such as the size of your clasp – that will influence the finished result. Get it right at the planning stage and not only will it look better, it will be quicker to make.

BALANCING YOUR COMPOSITION

The heaviest part of a necklace will fall to the center front, so don't try and defy gravity and put your heaviest beads on the side rather than in the center, you'll only be annoyed when it doesn't work. This doesn't mean you have to have a symmetrical composition, just that the weight needs to be balanced either side of the center.

GIVING GIFTS

You may want to give your beaded creations to friends and family. When planning, remember to think about the person's age, size, and taste. For example, your eight-year-old niece will only have a little wrist. Therefore, choose small, light beads to make her a bracelet. For a work colleague, you can make something more substantial and stylish. Ask yourself – will she like sophisticated or funky?

1 Work out what length you want your finished bracelet or necklace to be. You can do this by measuring your wrist or neck, or an existing piece of jewelry that fits well.

2 Decide what clasp you are going to use and measure it. Make sure you measure how long the clasp will be when CLOSED. So, if you want a finished necklace length of 17" (43 cm), and the clasp is 1½" (4 cm), and the crimps are ½" (1 cm), you would need to thread a string of beads 15½" (38 cm) long onto a piece of flexible wire 18½" (46 cm) long (see diagram below).

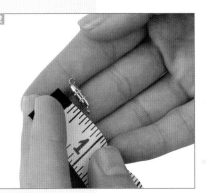

3 Once you know the length of beads required, you can get out your beads – and bead board if you have one – and begin designing. Lay your beads on the board in the groove and use the measurements shown to make sure you get an accurate length.

4 Once you are happy with your design, string it using flexible wire with crimps to secure the clasp. The result – a beautiful piece of jewelry!

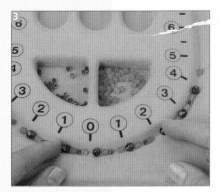

DETERMINING WIRE LENGTH

Finished length	–	Clasp	–	Crimps	+	3" (8 cm)	=	length of wire

Crimping

When you string a piece of jewelry onto flexible beading wire, you need to make sure the findings are securely attached so that the piece will last you a long time. The way to do this is to use crimps, which are small metal beads or tubes. When squashed, a crimp bites into the nylon coating of the wire and holds it tight.

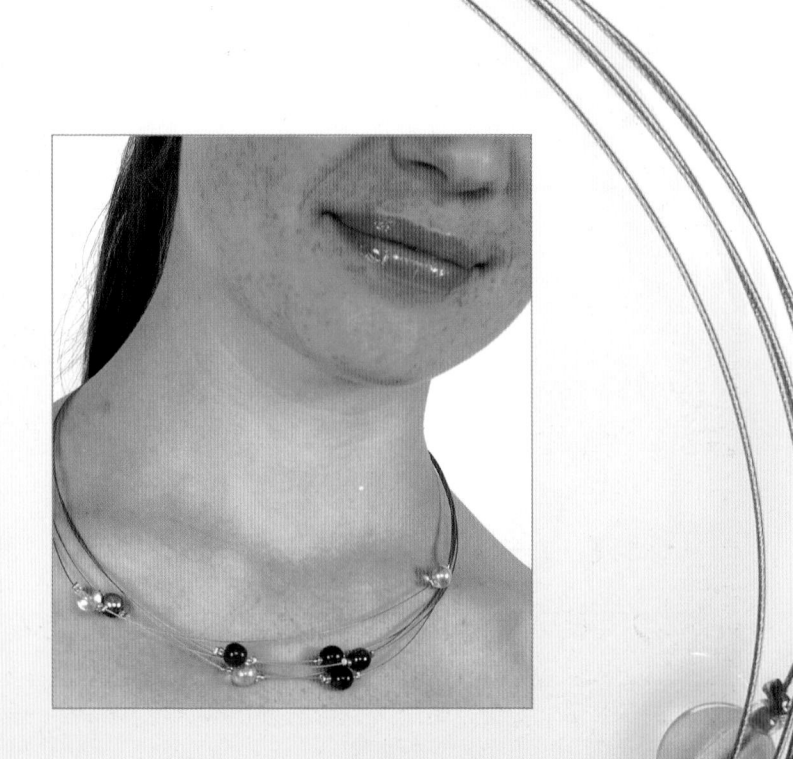

You can use flat or snipe nose pliers to squash the crimps. Or, if you plan to do a lot of crimping, it's worth investing in a pair of crimping pliers. These specially designed pliers will give you a rounder, smoother crimp, which looks more attractive and feels more comfortable. But they are more complicated to use. Whatever method you choose to use, do make sure you practice crimping before you try it on an actual project.

BUYING CRIMPS

Use the right size crimp for the flexible wire and crimping pliers you are using. A wrong sized crimp will either not grip the wire or will break when you squash it. If you are not sure, ask your bead seller for advice.

USING FLAT OR SNIPE NOSE PLIERS

1. Thread the flexible wire through a crimp, through the clasp and then back through the crimp.

2. Place the crimp into the jaws of the pliers and squeeze them shut to ensure the crimp bites into the wire.

3. Pull gently on the wire to check that the crimp has held.

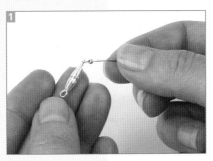

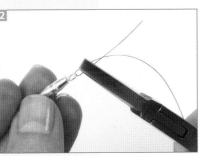

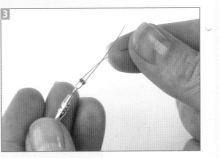

USING CRIMPING PLIERS

1. Thread the flexible wire through a crimp, through the clasp, and then back through the crimp.

2. Place the crimp into the notch in the crimping pliers that is nearest the handle. This is the one that squashes the crimp flat. Make sure that the two lengths of wire lie side by side and are not crossed inside the crimp. Gently squeeze the pliers shut. This will crimp the bead so it holds the wire. Pull gently on the wire to check that the crimp has held.

3. Now place the crimp into the notch in the pliers farthest away from the handle. You are now going to fold the crimp over so it returns to a more rounded shape. Ensure that the crimp sits in the notch vertically so that one wire sits above the other.

4. Gently close the pliers and the crimp will have been folded in half and rounded.

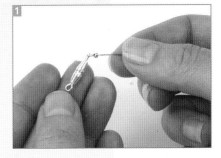

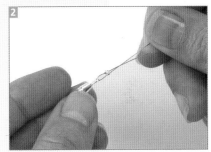

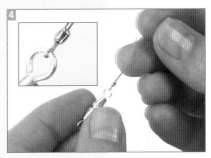

Using crimps with flexible beading wire

Flexible beading wire, which is sold under many different brand names, is the perfect stringing material for most jewelry projects. Made up of many fine strands of steel coated in nylon, it is pliant and strong. However, it cannot be knotted, so you need to use crimps to secure it. Once correctly secured, your jewelry will stand up to the test of time and you can wear it for years to come.

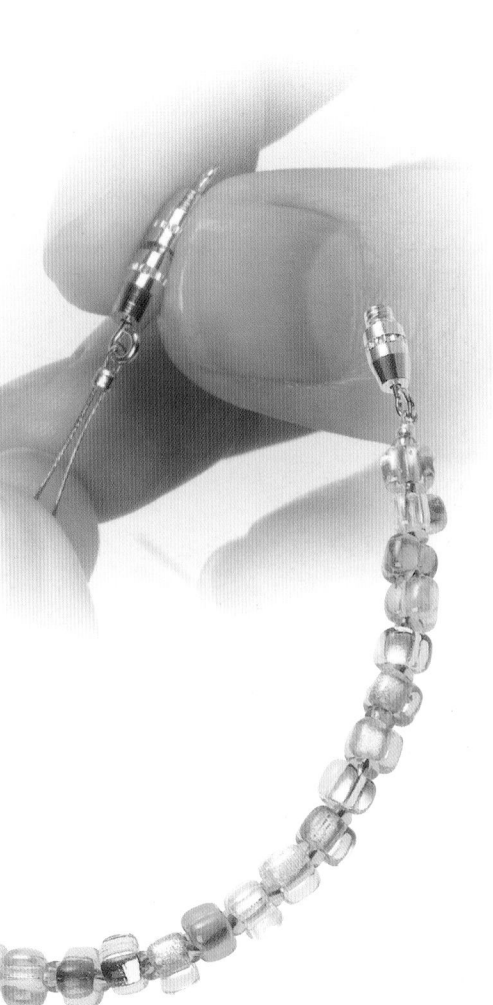

KINKY JEWELRY

Despite its many advantages, flexible beading wire can kink. And, once kinked, it stays that way. So be careful how you store or transport your finished jewelry. Try and keep it flat and uncoiled.

1 Following the guidance on pages 14–15, cut an appropriate length of flexible wire for your project.

2 Thread the wire through a crimp, the first part of the clasp, and then back through the crimp, so that there is about 1" (2.5 cm) of wire through the crimp. Using the technique described on page 17, close the crimp. Always make sure you leave a little space between the crimp and the clasp so that the clasp is free to move. If it is too tight, the clasp will rub against the wire, which could wear it down.

3 Trim the end of the wire to leave a short tail, which will be hidden under the beads. Gently pull the wire to ensure the crimp has held.

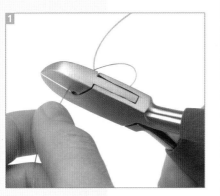

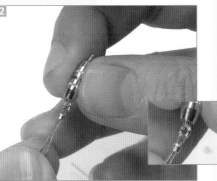

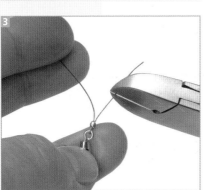

4 Begin threading on beads, making sure you cover both ends of the wire with beads. Add beads until you reach the required length, then thread on a crimp and the second half of the clasp.

5 Take the end of the wire back through the crimp and through a few of the beads in the design. Pull the wire so that the clasp sits up as tight as possible to the crimp.

6 Trim the wire as close as possible to the beads and then tug very gently on the clasp so that the end of the wire is pulled into the beads and the clasp now sits away from the crimp and can move. Close this crimp to secure, and gently pull on the clasp to ensure it has held tight.

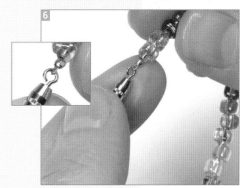

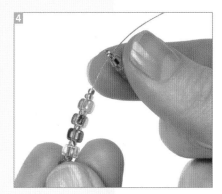

PROJECT

SIMPLY SHELLS

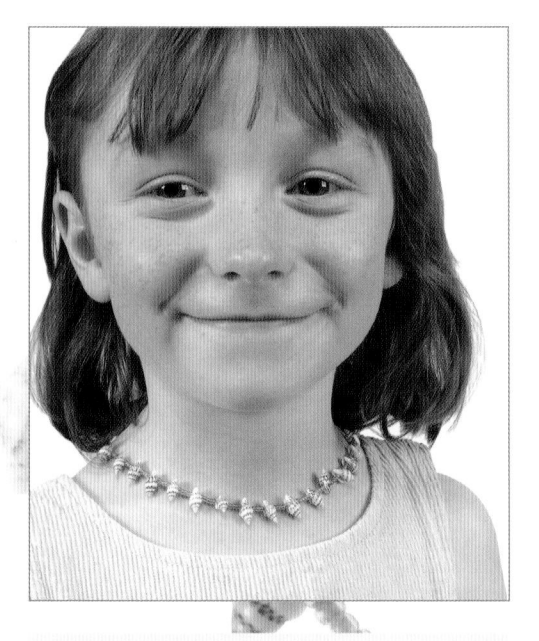

This single-strand necklace uses shell beads and matching seed beads to create a fun, summery look. It's quick and easy to make and can be done with any beads you have. On the following page you will see other examples to inspire you, but have a look through the rest of the book for bead combinations that appeal to you.

NOTIONS/TOOLS
+ *Wire cutters*
+ *Crimping, flat or snipe nose pliers*
+ *Measuring tape*

MATERIALS
+ *1 lobster clasp*
+ *1 split ring*
+ *5 g size 11 seed beads*
+ *40 shell beads*
+ *A length of flexible beading wire (see pages 14–15 to work out the length required)*
+ *2 crimps*

1 Decide how long you want the finished necklace to be (see pages 14–15) and cut a length of wire accordingly.

2 Attach one end of the wire to the lobster clasp using a crimp. Thread on 5 seed beads, making sure they cover both pieces of the flexible beading wire, followed by 1 shell bead. Continue threading using a repeating pattern of 5 seed beads and 1 shell bead.

3 Once you have threaded on the required length of beads and shells, attach the other end of the wire to the split ring using a crimp.

4 The split ring will fasten neatly and securely to the lobster clasp.

VARIATIONS

This technique is incredibly versatile and you'll be surprised at how different a necklace can look simply by changing the size, color, or shape of the beads you use. Play around with the beads you have to come up with different combinations. You can use your bead board, if you have one, to lay designs out until you are happy with them.

WATCHBAND

This watchband has Chinese metal beads and seed beads threaded on flexible beading wire, which is secured with crimps to the watch face and the clasp. The toggle and ring clasp makes it easy to put the watch on. You can "fine tune" the length of the band by varying the number of seed beads you use, so the band will fit you perfectly.

MATERIALS

+ *1 watch face with "rings" to attach the band (avoid watch faces with "pin" attachments)*
+ *8–12 beads with a flat profile, approx ½" (12 mm) diameter. We used Chinese metal beads with an enamel finish*
+ *1 toggle and loop clasp*
+ *A few size 8 seed beads*
+ *A length of flexible beading wire at least 8" (20 cm) longer than your wrist circumference*
+ *4 crimps*

NOTIONS/TOOLS

+ *Wire cutters*
+ *Crimping, flat or snipe nose pliers*
+ *Measuring tape*

1 Thread a crimp onto one end of the beading wire and pass the wire through the ring at the base of the watch face and back through the crimp. Close the crimp as described on page 17.

2 Place the watch face on your arm and measure from the ring at the base of the watch to the center of your inner wrist. Add approximately 3" (7 cm) to this measurement and cut the wire.

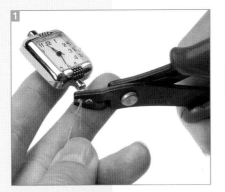

You'll find you keep getting asked for the time when you wear one of these gorgeous watchbands – and they string up so quickly you could make one for every outfit.

3 Thread on 1 seed bead and the Chinese metal beads to the length you require, then 2 more seed beads (see box, below). Thread on a crimp and pass the wire through the toggle half of the clasp and back through the crimp and a few beads on the watchband. Pull everything up as tight as you can.

4 Trim the end of wire, relax the wire a little and close the crimp.

5 Repeat from step 1 on the other side of the watch face, using the ring half of the clasp. Be particularly careful in determining the length you need.

DETERMINING LENGTH

Using 4 Chinese beads and just 3 seed beads gave us a length of 3" (8.5 cm) for one side of the band, once the toggle clasp had been added. Each additional Chinese bead will give an extra ½" (12 mm). If you need to fine tune the length, use extra seed beads, either next to the watch face and clasp, or in between the Chinese beads.

SEMI-PRECIOUS STRANDS

This simple technique makes a beautiful necklace that can be worn in many different ways. By making three strands that are left unjoined, you can wear all three individually, as pairs, or all together. Braid or twist the three strands together and you have two more styles to choose from – and you can always add extra strands as you buy more beads!

MATERIALS
✦ 1 S-hook clasp
✦ 6 split rings or jump rings
✦ 3 strands of semi-precious beads
  (strands can vary in length but are
  generally 15–17" (38–43 cm) long)
✦ 5 g of matching seed beads
✦ 3 lengths of flexible beading wire
✦ 6 crimps

NOTIONS/TOOLS
✦ Wire cutters
✦ Crimping, flat or snipe nose pliers
✦ Measuring tape

1 Decide how long you want the finished strands to be (see pages 14–15), and cut three lengths of wire accordingly. Remember to allow for the split or jump rings at both ends and the S-hook clasp. Using a crimp, attach one end of a length of wire to one of the rings.

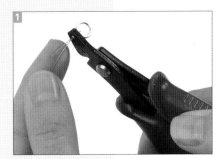

Using semi-precious beads (as we have in the project) makes this necklace feel very special, but you can mix and match the beads you use as you wish. Experiment with texture and color – you can make some really eye-catching pieces using this technique.

2 Once you have calculated the length of beads you need to string, check if the strands of semi-precious beads are long enough. If they are too short, you will need to add in some seed beads to make up the length. Work out the length of seed beads you require, if any, and decide whether you are going to add these right along the strand or would prefer to have them all at the ends where they will be less visible. Begin threading on the beads, making sure they cover both pieces of the flexible beading wire.

3 When the strand is long enough, attach the remaining end to a split or jump ring with a crimp. Repeat steps 1–3 with the other two strands.

4 Once all the strands are made, simply slip the rings onto each end of your S-hook. Wear as many or as few as you like.

Opening & closing jump rings

Jump rings are metal rings that are used to attach findings and clasps, and can also be linked to each other to make chains. Make sure you open and close the jump rings correctly to help them retain their shapes. For security, they must be closed leaving as small a gap as possible. You can also use this technique for opening and closing the loops on findings.

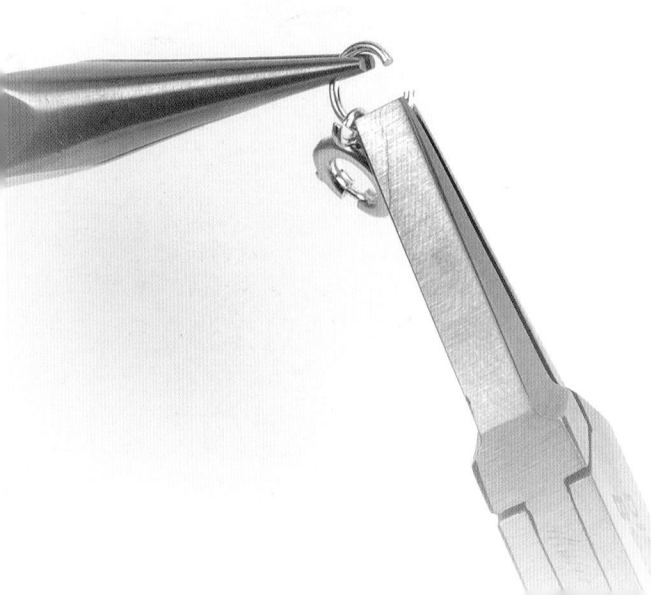

You will need to use two pairs of pliers to open and close the rings successfully. It is better to use flat or snipe nose pliers, as they have flat inner jaws that will help you grip the rings and control them better.

It's always advisable to practice your jump ring technique before making your finished piece, as creating a few broken and bent jump rings at this point is better than losing a cherished piece of jewelry due to a jump ring that wasn't quite closed.

With simple jump ring chains you can really give the "wow" factor to some dramatic, colorful beads, showing them off to their best advantage.

27

1 Hold the jump ring with two pairs of pliers, one on each side of the join in the ring.

2 Slowly push one hand forward while pulling the other toward you. Do this until the gap in the ring is large enough for you to use.

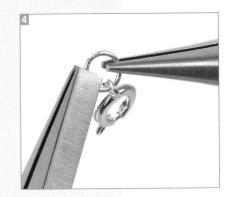

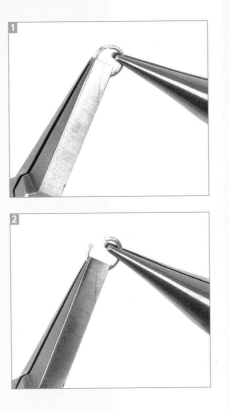

3 Once opened, put the jump ring through the hole or loop in your finding, or through another jump ring if you are making a chain. You can, if you wish, put a bead on the jump ring at this stage.

4 To close the jump ring so that it keeps its shape, simply hold the ring as before and reverse the pulling and pushing you did to open it. Bring the two ends together and slightly past each other so that when you release the ring there is as little a gap as possible.

Jump ring chains make interesting jewelry in their own right. Add beads and they become really special.

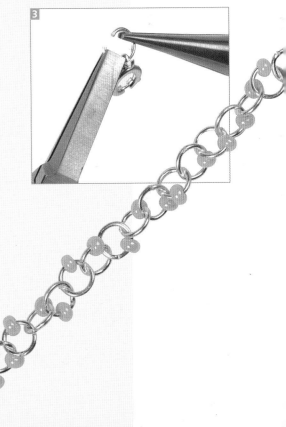

BAD TECHNIQUE

DO NOT open the ring by pulling the cut ends away from each other in the same plane, as shown in photo a, as it will not return to its original round shape. Open it by pulling and pushing the ends apart, as shown in photo b.

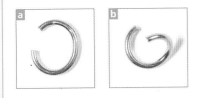

Designing & planning earrings

When planning your earrings, your first thought will be how pretty your beads are and how much you want to use them. But to get the end result you want, you need to take some other things into account.

MIX AND MATCH

Five of the projects in this book feature earrings, each using a different technique. Remember to look at them each time you make one of the other projects and think about whether you can use beads left over from, say, your bracelet or necklace to make matching earrings. So, if you string a necklace you can use some of the same beads and thread them on flexible wire or head pins for earrings that complement the necklace. You can also adapt some of the other projects to make earrings to match. For example, if you make the charm bracelet on pages 80–81, why not make two more charms and turn them into earrings?

For example, you need to think about the length and style you prefer. These are discussed on the next page. Most important of all, be prepared to play with your beads and experiment until you are happy with your design.

CHOOSING YOUR MATERIALS

When choosing your beads, probably the most important consideration is their weight. A bead's size is not necessarily an indication of how much it weighs. For example, glass is heavier than plastic. And some large beads are hollow and much lighter than they look. So pick your beads up and think about their weight in relation to your ear lobe!

Decide what color threading materials will suit your beads best. Then make sure you have earring findings to match.

Check the holes of your beads, especially if using head pins. If the bead holes are so large that the head pin will slip through, remember to buy a small bead to thread on first to prevent this.

DESIGNING YOUR EARRINGS

The first thing to consider is the finished length you want. Remember that the earring consists of two parts: the dangle(s) and the finding.

Decide how many dangles you want. The number you can fit on to the finding will be limited by the size of its loop. If you want many dangles, you may find a hoop the best choice for you. The more dangles you have, the lighter the beads should be. For example, the earrings illustrated on the top use sequins with seed beads to get a full effect with little weight. The earrings on the bottom have only three dangles to compensate for the weight of the large glass beads.

If you are planning several dangles, be aware that smaller beads at the top of each one will allow them to hang closer together. If you want a "spiky" look, put large beads at the top.

Having collected your beads together, experiment with different arrangements. It's surprising how many different combinations you can create with just a few beads. To get an idea of how they will look, thread them onto pins to compare the results and see how they look when held up.

CRIMPED EARRINGS

These earrings are so quick to make you can have a pair for any occasion in just a few minutes. You can vary the beads and the length of the loop of wire to create different styles. You will be putting four lengths of flexible wire through the crimps, however, so this project is a little trickier to make than the earlier ones. If it doesn't work first time, don't worry, just cut the beads off and start again.

MATERIALS
+ 2 x 8 mm bi-cone crystals
+ 4 x 6 mm bi-cone crystals
+ 4 x 3 mm bi-cone crystals
+ Flexible beading wire
+ 4 crimps
+ 2 earring hooks

NOTIONS/TOOLS
+ Wire cutters
+ Measuring tape
+ Flat, snipe nose or
  crimping pliers

1 Decide how long you want your earrings to be, excluding the earring hooks. Cut a piece of flexible beading wire to twice that length plus 4" (10 cm). Thread on crystals in the following sequence: 1 small, 1 medium, 1 large, 1 medium, and 1 small.

2 Bring the two ends of the wire together and pass them through two crimps.

This style makes the most of beautiful beads. Chunks of crystal, for example, that are irregularly shaped and highly colorful look great when simply strung.

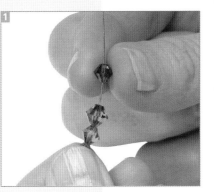

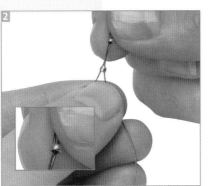

3 Bend the ends of the wire back and pass them together through the top crimp so that approximately ½" (1 cm) of wire is through the crimp. Adjust the top crimp until the top and bottom loops are the size you want, and pull the lower crimp down the lower loop so that it is about ½" (1 cm) away from the top crimp. Close the top crimp.

4 Trim the ends of the wire to ¹⁄₁₆" (2 mm). Carefully bring the lower crimp over the ends of the wire and close the crimp so that the ends of the wire are hidden inside it. This is where a little practice may be necessary to get a neat finish.

5 Open the loop of the earring hook (see pages 26–7), place the top loop of the earring into the hook and close the hook. Make a second earring to match.

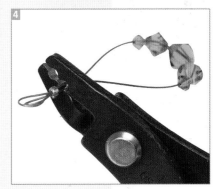

PROJECT   MULTI-STRAND CHOKER

This fabulous choker would be great on that special evening out. It makes use of several strands of beads and spacer bars to hold the beads separate and in line. By adding a chain to one end, the choker is adjustable and you can wear it at slightly different lengths. This is also useful if you are making it for a gift or when your friends ask to borrow it!

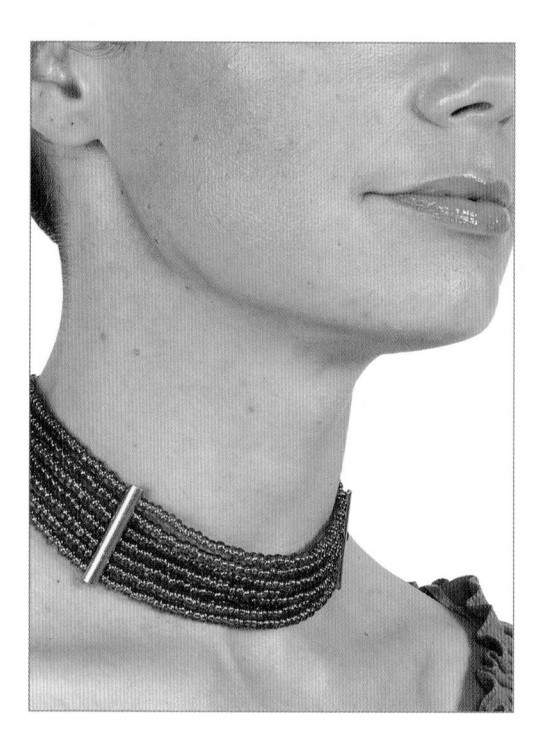

MATERIALS
+ 2 x 7-hole end bars
+ 2 x 7-hole spacer bars to match the
  end bars
+ 1 lobster clasp
+ 20 jump rings
+ 50 g size 6 seed beads
+ 7 lengths of flexible beading wire
  (see pages 14–15 to work out the
  length required)
+ 14 crimps

NOTIONS/TOOLS
+ Wire cutters
+ Crimping, flat or snipe nose pliers
+ Measuring tape

1 Decide how long you want the strands on the choker to be (see pages 14–15) and taking into account both the end bars and the spacer bars, cut seven pieces of flexible beading wire to this length. Attach each to a separate hole on one of the end bars using crimps.

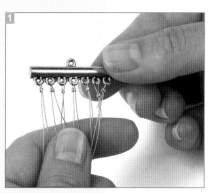

This three-strand variation is subtle and sophisticated. The spacer bars used here are etched and give another dimension to this otherwise simple choker.

2 Determine the length of beads to thread on and divide this by three. This new measurement is how long each section of beading will be between the spacer bars. Begin threading the first third of the beads onto each wire until you reach this length, then thread on the first spacer bar.

3 Continue threading the beads, adding the second spacer bar when the next third of the beads are on, until the choker is the length you need. Use crimps to secure all of the wires to the other end bar.

4 Once the choker is beaded, attach the lobster clasp to one end bar using 3 jump rings. Use the rest of the jump rings to make a chain and attach it to the other end bar.

STAY IN CONTROL

Handling several strands of beads at once can be taxing, even for experienced beaders. Keep control of the strands by using masking tape to anchor each one to your work surface as you complete it. This way the beads won't roll off your wires as you work.

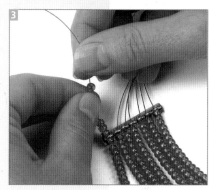

SPARKLING STRANDS

This stunning necklace brings together many different shapes and sizes of beads. The combination of aqua, turquoise, teal and other shades of blue evokes the sparkling Caribbean Sea. We have used end bars to help keep the different strands separate. This helps the necklace hang beautifully, so each different strand can be enjoyed.

MATERIALS

÷ 2 x 3-hole end bars, with clasp attached, if available
÷ 1 clasp (if there isn't one attached to the end bars)
÷ 2 jump rings to attach clasp to the end bars, if necessary
÷ 10 g size 11 seed beads
÷ Approximately 100 g of mixed Czech glass beads
÷ 6 lengths of flexible beading wire (see pages 14–15 to work out length required)
÷ 12 crimp beads

NOTIONS/TOOLS

÷ Wire cutters
÷ Crimping, flat or snipe nose pliers
÷ Measuring tape

1 Decide how long you want the shortest strand of the necklace to be (see pages 14–15); cut a piece of flexible beading wire to this length. Then cut another 5 lengths of wire, each 1½" (4 cm) longer than the previous one. The last length will be 7½" (20 cm) longer than the first. Using a crimp, attach one end of the first piece of wire to the top hole in one of the end bars.

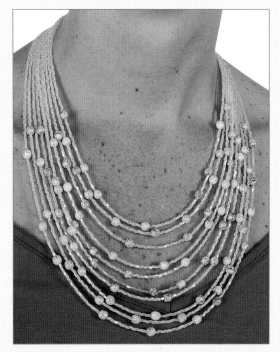

This version is very different in style to our project. The strands of tiny, twinkly white beads carry "floating" round glass beads. The end bars for this necklace have five holes each and we have used two strands to each hole. Each length of cable is 1" (2.5 cm) longer than the previous one.

2 Thread this strand with beads, mixing some seed beads in between each larger bead to separate them and keep the final necklace lighter.

3 Once the strand is completely beaded, attach the remaining end to the top hole of the other end bar.

4 Attach the second strand of wire to the same hole you have already used in one of the end bars. Thread beads onto this second strand until it is 1½" (4 cm) longer than the first. Finish by crimping into the same hole as that already used on the other end bar. Continue adding 2 strands to each hole in the end bars until you have added a total of 6 strands, each 1½" (4 cm) longer than the previous one. Once the necklace is beaded, attach a clasp to the end bars, using jump rings (see page 26) to finish, if necessary.

Using leather & fabric cords

Leather thong or fabric cord make wonderful stringing materials, being both economical and easy to use. You will find they come in many colors and thicknesses, making them very versatile, and they can add interest to your jewelry designs.

When using cord, always remember the golden rule: the cord is always larger than you think and the holes in your beads are always smaller! So it's worth taking your beads along when you choose cord, or vice versa. Always test that they fit, making sure you test a few of the beads, as the holes may vary slightly. Remember to check that the cord will go through the beads the number of times you need it to for your particular project.

To attach cord to a clasp, you need cord crimps. These are little open "boxes" of metal with a loop at the end. When a cord crimp is closed over the end of a length of cord, it grips it securely.

Fabric cords can fray at the ends, making them tricky to thread through your beads. But if you first treat the cut end of the cord (see page 37), your threading will go a lot more smoothly. Leather cord does not fray, so you can just "cut and thread".

TREATING THE END OF FABRIC CORD

1 Paint craft glue or clear nail polish onto the end of your fabric cord (or dip the cord into the glue/nail polish). Make sure you cover at least the last 1½" (3 cm). Smooth off the excess glue or nail polish with your fingers. This helps to narrow and straighten the treated section. Leave the cord to dry completely.

2 When the cord is dry, using the sharpest scissors you have, trim the end to a point.

3 You can now use this needle-shaped end of your cord to thread through your beads more easily. Once the pointed end is through the bead, you can pull the rest through.

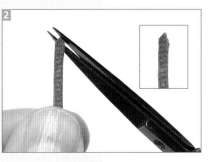

MEASURING FABRIC CORD

When you are planning your necklace or bracelet, make sure you allow for the length of treated fabric cord that will be trimmed off before fixing the cord crimps.

USING CORD CRIMPS

1 Cut your leather thong or fabric cord straight across at the end. If you have treated the fabric cord, trim off the treated section, except for the length of the cord crimp.

2 Put the end of the cord into the cord crimp so that it sits immediately under the loop of the crimp. Hold the cord, supporting the crimp with your index finger and with your thumb on top of the cord, just below the crimp.

3 Take your flat or snipe nose pliers and squeeze gently on the sides of the crimp so that they bend toward each other over the cord.

4 Now place the jaws of the pliers so that they hold the crimp from the other sides. Squeeze down firmly to close the crimp.

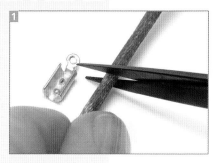

CORRECTION!

As long as the cord is held securely by the crimp, don't worry if a few stray threads escape from between the crimp's closed edges. Trim them away with a sharp craft knife.

Making overhand knots

Having threaded some beads onto leather thong or fabric cord, you can hold them in place using knots. The simple overhand knot is highly effective when you are working with a variety of beads and cords.

Quick and very easy to do, overhand knots make a feature of the pretty colored leather thong and satin cords you can buy. Think carefully when choosing the cords to go with your beads. The cord needs to go through the hole of the bead easily, but it also has to be thick enough to make a good-sized knot that won't slip back through the bead.

While making this knot is very easy, it can take practice to get it to sit in the right place. We have some advice for you about placing the knots exactly where you want them every time.

OVERHAND KNOT

1 Make a loop in the cord so that one end crosses over the other. Hold where they cross between your index finger and thumb.

2 Take the end that is lying on top and bring it through the loop from behind. Pull both ends of the cord gently, but do not tighten the knot.

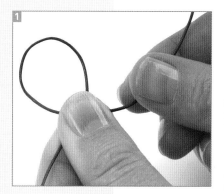

3 Gently push the knot to the exact position on the cord where you want it to sit. If you are making your knot before threading on a bead, hold one end of the cord immediately behind the knot with one hand, then pull on the other end of the cord with your other hand to tighten the knot. As you pull the cord, push against the knot with your index finger and thumb so that the knot ends up sitting between your two thumbs.

4 If you want the knot to be right up against a bead, make the knot as close to it as you can. Then tighten the knot by pulling on the end of the cord while pushing the knot toward the bead with your finger and thumb.

POSITIONING AN OVERHAND KNOT

To move an overhand knot to the correct position before you tighten it, place the tip of a large sewing needle into the center of the knot and use the needle to drag the knot along. This ensures that the knot doesn't close too soon.

PROJECT **KNOTTED CORD BRACELET**

One thing to remember when working with satin cord is that the cord is always thicker than you think and the holes in your beads are always smaller than you think! If you can, take your beads with you when choosing your cord to make sure they work together. Treating the ends of your cord using the techniques on pages 36–7 will help you thread the cord more easily.

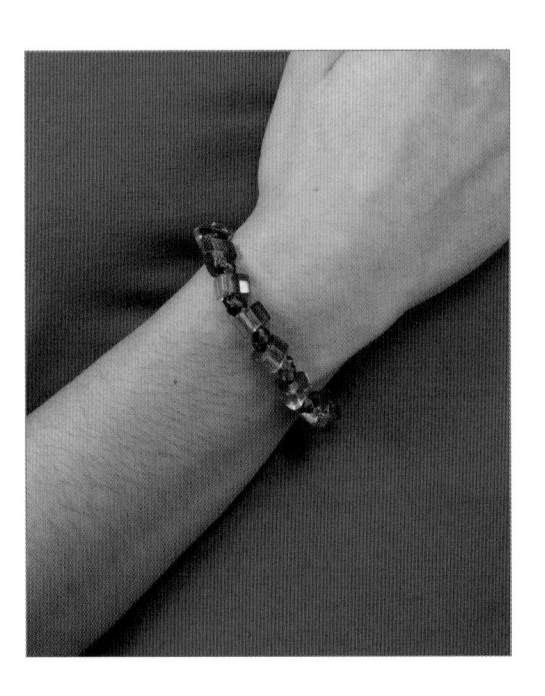

MATERIALS
- 2 different colors of satin cord/rattail to fit through your beads. See step 1 (below) for advice on length
- Approximately 15 glass beads
- 2 cord crimps
- 1 clasp to attach to cord crimps
- 2 jump rings for attaching clasp

NOTIONS/TOOLS
- Scissors
- Glue or clear nail polish (optional)
- Measuring tape
- Flat or snipe nose pliers

1. Decide how long you want your bracelet to be. It is worth laying your beads out and planning this project before you buy or cut your cord. Decide how you want your beads to lie and how many knots you will have. Each knot will take up nearly 1" (2 cm), depending on how thick the cord is and how tight you tie it. You will need to take all this into account when buying your cord.

2. Attach one end of each of your two cords to one of your cord crimps, making sure it is holding both pieces tightly and is firmly shut.

3. Begin threading on your beads and knotting the two cords together as required, creating your bracelet. This is a simple overhand knot (see pages 38–9), knotting both pieces of cord together.

4. Once it is the length you require, attach the other cord ending. Then, using your jump rings, join the clasp on to finish.

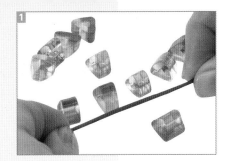

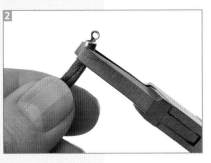

VARIATIONS

This simple technique can be extended to make a matching necklace. Alternatively, you could space the beads out more, or use more knots than beads for a totally different look.

This simple variation uses more beads and only one length of cord.

LEATHER THONG BELT

This pretty belt, made with brightly colored leather thong and chunky beads, makes an easy-to-wear fashion accessory. Be careful when choosing your beads. The large beads that form the main part of the belt must have holes big enough to take three strands of cord. The smaller beads that form the fringes have only one cord threaded through each.

MATERIALS

÷ Leather thong, 1 mm thick. See step 1 for the length you need
÷ 30–40 large glass beads, each approximately ½" (1 cm) across and with large holes
÷ Collection of small glass beads, approximately 40–50 g

NOTIONS/TOOLS

÷ Scissors
÷ Measuring tape
÷ Masking tape

1. Determine the sizes of the leather thongs. First take your waist measurement. Multiply this by two to ensure you have a generous allowance for making the knots. Add 4" (10 cm) to allow for the space where the two ends of the belt tie together. Add a further 10" (25 cm) for the fringes and cut the first thong to this length. Cut the second thong 2" (5 cm) longer than the first. Cut a third thong 4" (10 cm) longer than the first.

2. Fold each length of thong in half to find the center point. Hold all three lengths of cord together at the center and wrap a piece of masking tape tightly around them.

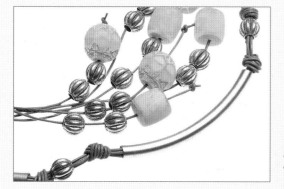

This variation has all the funky chic of the leather thong, but the silver beads and tube add an elegant touch for a more "evening" feel.

3. With all three lengths of cord together, make an overhand knot and position it 8" (20 cm) from the end of the shortest length. Remove the tape.

4. Pass the long ends of the thong through a large bead and bring the bead down to sit against the knot. Make a new overhand knot with all three lengths and position it about 1" (2.5 cm) away from the previous knot. The bead will be held loosely in place between the two knots.

5. Continue adding large beads and knotting between them, spacing the knots evenly along the belt. Check the belt for length as you go – the allowance for knotting is generous. Once you have tied your final knot, trim the ends of the remaining lengths of thong to match the other end of the belt.

6. Thread about 5" (12.5 cm) small beads onto one of the lengths of thong. Tie an overhand knot close to the end to hold the beads in place. Repeat with the other five ends.

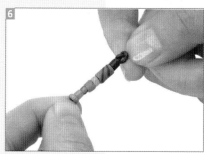

Making twist knots with cord

This knot is more decorative than the overhand knot and enables you to create a thicker cord from two finer ones. As you tie more knots on top of each other you will create a spiral.

If you have ever done any macramé, you will already be familiar with this knot. (In macramé books, it is usually called a half hitch.) You can place beads into your knotted cord as you make it. One way is to put beads in between sections of knotting (see the hair barrette on page 46). Or you can put smaller beads into the knots themselves as you make them (see the knotted leather bracelet on page 48).

Your first job will be to choose your two cords. One is the inner cord and the other is the cord you will be using to make the knots. The cords do not have to be the same thickness – you will get good results with two cords the same thickness, or with a fine cord knotted over a thicker one. Here, we have used a soft embroidery thread knotted over a linen cord.

THRIFTY CORDS

The knotting will very largely cover the cord you knot over. So you might decide to use some cord left over from another project for the inner cord. It will be visible in the loop before the knotting starts and little specks of color from it are bound to show through the knotting, so bear that in mind when choosing your threads.

1 Decide on the length of the finished knotted cord you want. Cut the **inner cord** to that length, adding 2" (5 cm) (and an allowance for finishing, depending on your project). You will need approximately 10 times more of the **knotting cord** than the inner cord. This may be very long, so wind the knotting cord round a small piece of card or a bobbin so that you can hold it more easily and not get in a tangle. Bring the ends of the inner cord and knotting cord together and tie them in an overhand knot close to the ends.

2 You need to fix the work so that you can pull against it and have both hands free. You can do this by pinning the knot to a pin board or taping it to the edge of your tabletop with masking tape.

These steps are given for a right-handed person. If you are left-handed, reverse the directions.

3 Hold the inner cord in your left hand, supporting it with your fourth and little fingers. Take the knotting cord off the card in your right hand and pass it over the top of the inner cord. Hold the knotting cord in position with your left thumb. Keep

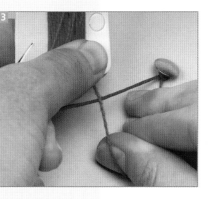

a loop open with the thumb and fingers of your right hand.

4 Pass the card under the inner cord and through the loop, giving it back to your right hand and taking it with your thumb and index finger. Now take the knotting cord between the thumb and first finger of your left hand so that it lies over the top of the inner cord. Bring the whole length of the knotting cord through the loop.

5 Pull on the knotting cord to tighten the knot. As you tighten the knot, pull it as far up the inner cord as it will go.

6 Continue making knots (by repeating steps 3, 4, 5 and 6) until the knotting is the length you require. As you go along, you will find that the knots start to spiral around the inner cord. Make sure you bring each new knot right up to the last one.

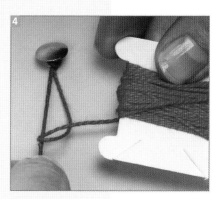

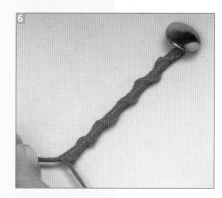

BEADED CORD BARRETTE

If you make several of these strands, varying the length and thicknesses of the cords, you can wear them singly or several together, like our model. A length of colorful ribbon attached to the barrette gives it a little more pizazz.

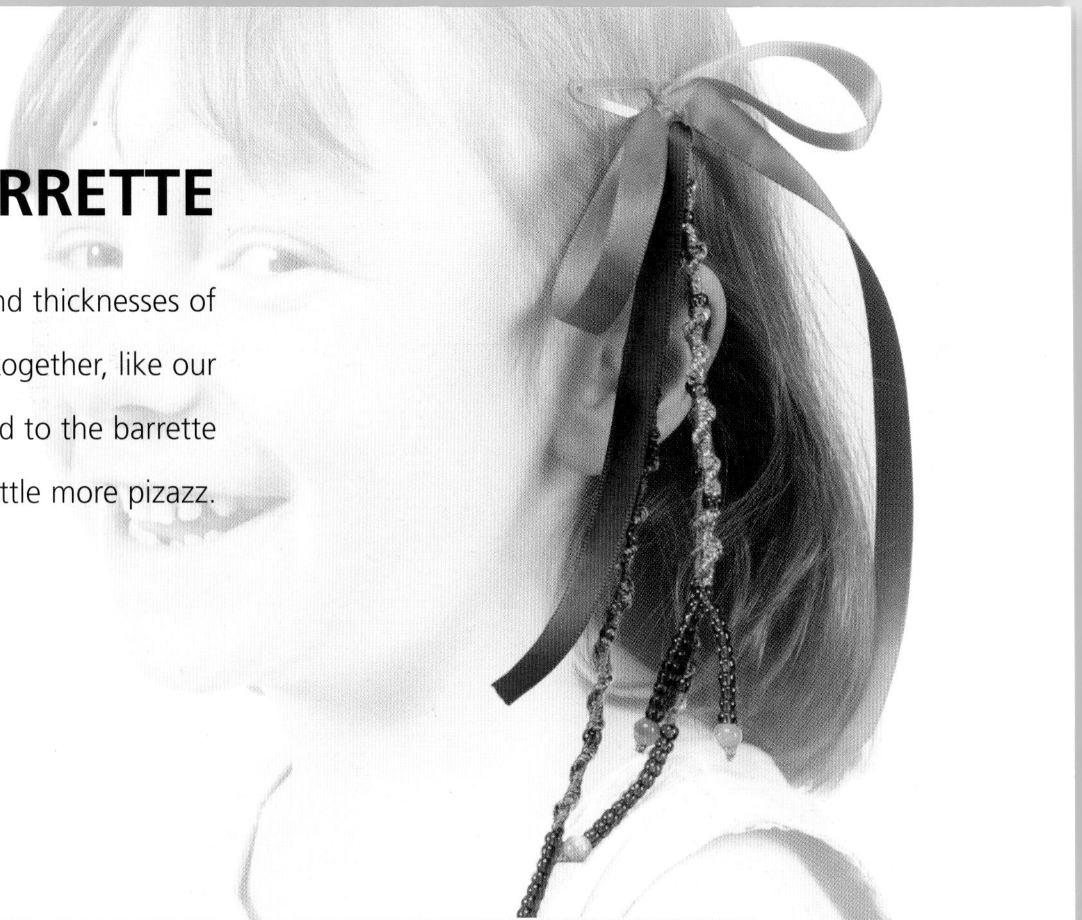

MATERIALS (for each strand)
+ 1 jump ring
+ Approximately 20 pony beads or size 6 seed beads
+ Embroidery thread (see step 1 for lengths to cut)
+ 5 mm round glass bead
+ 1 barrette
+ Length of ribbon (optional)

NOTIONS/TOOLS
+ Scissors
+ Measuring tape
+ Pin board and thumb tack, or masking tape
+ Craft glue or clear nail polish
+ Small piece of card or a bobbin

1 Decide how long you want the finished piece to be. Add 4" (10 cm) and cut a piece of embroidery thread twice this length. This is your **inner cord**. Decide how long you want the knotted section (above the beaded fringe) to be. Multiply that length by 10, add the length of the fringe and a further 2" (5 cm). Cut a second piece of thread to twice the total length. This is your **knotting cord**. Fold both cords in the center and push the folds together through the jump ring so there is a loop of about 1" (2.5 cm). Bring all four ends of thread through the loop and pull down to tighten the threads onto the jump ring.

2 Pin the jump ring onto the pin board, or tape it to your table top. Treat approximately 1" (2.5 cm) of all the ends with craft glue or clear nail polish to make threading on beads easier. Wind the knotting cord around a piece of card to make a "bobbin". Hold the inner cord in your left hand. Take the card in your right hand, pass it over the top of the inner cord and into your left hand, taking it with your thumb and index finger. Keep a loop open with the thumb and fingers of your right hand.

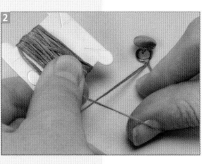

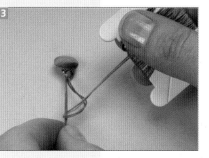

3 Pass the card under the inner cord and through the loop, giving it back to your right hand and taking it with your thumb and index finger.

4 Pull the knotting cord gently up the inner cord until it reaches the jump ring and pull the knot tight.

5 Repeat steps 3–4 until you have about 1" (2.5 cm) of knotting completed. Unwind the knotting cord from the card and pass all four threads through a size 6 seed bead. Rewind the knotting cord onto the card.

6 Continue making sections of knotting and adding beads until you have the length you want (excluding the fringe). Pass all four threads through your fringe beads, ending with the large round glass bead. Make an overhand knot with all the threads and position it as close as possible to the last bead.

7 Trim off the excess threads close to the knot and treat them with a dab of craft glue or clear nail polish to secure. Attach the jump ring to the inside arm of the barrette. Repeat steps for as many strands as you require and add a length of colorful ribbon to finish if you wish.

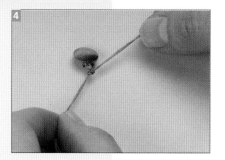

PROJECT

LEATHER BRACELET

We have used fine leather cord for this bracelet, which means it works up good and fast. Each half of the clasp is attached before you start knotting and then the two ends of the bracelet are knotted together in the center leaving some fun fringe to dangle.

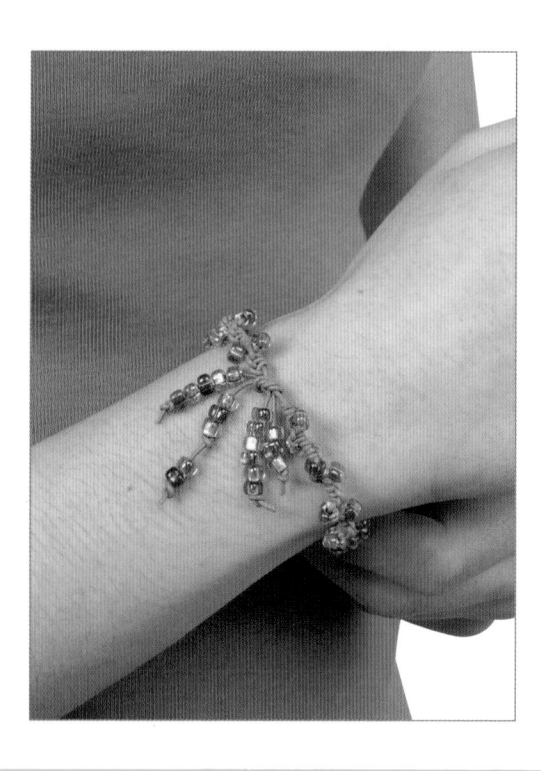

MATERIALS

÷ *Approximately 30 pony beads or size 6 seed beads*
÷ *Fine leather thong (see below for lengths to cut)*
÷ *1 loop and toggle clasp*

NOTIONS/TOOLS

÷ *Scissors*
÷ *Measuring tape*
÷ *Pin board and thumb tack or masking tape*

1 Decide how long you want your bracelet to be. You will be working on one half of the bracelet at a time, so measure the clasp, take that measurement away from the finished length and divide by two. This is length A. Multiply length A by 11, add 4" (10 cm) and cut a piece of leather thong to that length. Measure length A from one end of the thong, add 4" (10 cm) and fold the thong at this point. Push the folded thong through the ring of your clasp and pass both the long and short ends of the thong through the loop to fix it onto the clasp.

2 Pin the clasp to the pin board, or tape it to your tabletop. Thread half your beads onto the long end of the thong and tie an overhand knot at the end of the cord to hold the beads on it.

3 Follow the directions given on page 45 to make three twist knots. Pull all the beads through the loop of each knot as you make it.

4 Bring the first bead up to the last knot made. Make a twist knot to hold the bead in place as close as possible to the last knot.

5 Make three more twist knots. Now bring up the next bead. Secure it in place with a twist knot. Repeat this sequence – three knots, bead, three knots, bead – until the knotted section of this half of the bracelet is the length required (i.e. length A), ending with three twist knots. Repeat from step 1 to make the second half of the bracelet. Join the two halves of the bracelet together with a square knot (see page 51).

6 Thread a few beads onto one of the four ends of thong. Tie an overhand knot to hold the beads in place and trim the thong close to the knot. Decorate the other three thong ends in the same way, making each fringe a slightly different length and varying the number of beads you use for each.

This is a versatile technique that you can adapt and refine to your own taste as you become more practiced.

Knotting elastic cord

Elastic cord is great for making quick, funky pieces of jewelry. Because it stretches, the pieces don't need a clasp and can be simply pulled on over the wrist, which means you don't have to worry too much about the size of the finished piece if you are making it for a friend. To finish it, the cord is knotted. There are two different knots you can use – the choice of which is up to you. You can try both types and see which one best suits your purpose.

TESTING YOUR KNOTS

Always test that your knots have held by gently tugging on them. If they haven't held it will be obvious and you will need to tie them again.

OVERHAND KNOT

This is the basic knot that you are probably used to tying; just make sure you keep both ends of the cord together. It is easier to tie than a square knot but can be bulkier and therefore harder to hide.

1. Bring the two ends of your cord together so that they lay side by side, make a loop and then pull the ends through.

2. Once you're happy that the knot is secure, trim the ends.

NOT ENOUGH STRETCH

When tying your cord ends together, make sure you never pull the elastic too tight, as when you come to wear the piece there will be no stretch left in the elastic to get it over your hand.

SQUARE KNOT

This knot is slightly trickier to tie but can be more easily slipped inside your beads to hide it.

1. Lay the two ends of your elastic cord facing each other. Then take the left hand side cord over the right, and then up through the central loop.

2. Next, take the cord end that's now on the right, lay this over the cord on the left, then bring it up through the central loop. Pull on the ends of the cord to tighten the knot, then trim the cord ends and hide the knot inside one of your beads.

BAD TECHNIQUE

Make sure you follow the instructions for this knot carefully and use the correct side of cord to lay over the other, as if you don't you will tie a knot that does not hold.

SIMPLE BUT STYLISH

This simple and versatile bracelet and ring set uses elastic cord to make jewelry that can be slipped on over your wrist and finger easily. This also means that it can be worn by anyone who has a problem using clasps.

MATERIALS

+ *Elastic cord*
+ *Approximately 45–60 round glass beads*
+ *A scattering of seed beads to match*

NOTIONS/TOOLS

+ *Scissors*
+ *Measuring tape*

1 Decide how long you want your bracelet to be (make sure you leave at least 2" (5 cm) extra to help you knot the cord to secure) and cut the elastic cord to this length.

2 Thread on your beads until you reach the length you need. Then knot your cord using either of the knots described on pages 50–51. When you're sure the knots are secure, trim the cord ends and hide them within the beads by tucking them back into the holes.

3 Make a matching ring. To make this comfortable to wear, use seed beads to go around your finger and one or two round glass beads as a focal point at the front of the ring in which to hide the knot.

TEST YOUR STRETCH

Remember, when tying the cord ends together, make sure you don't pull the elastic too tightly as this will reduce the elasticity in the bracelet or ring. When you come to wear the piece there will be no stretch left in the elastic to get it over your hand.

VARIATIONS

This technique is incredibly versatile and you'll be surprised at how different a necklace can look simply by changing the size, color, or shape of the beads you use. Play around with the beads you have to come up with different combinations.

BAREFOOT SANDALS & HAND ORNAMENT

These sandals are great for the summer and can be made in brightly colored beads to catch the sun. If you plan on wearing them on the beach or at the poolside, make them with plastic beads so there's no chance of any color running. As these are made on elastic cord you don't need to be too exact with your measurements, they will stretch to fit anyone!

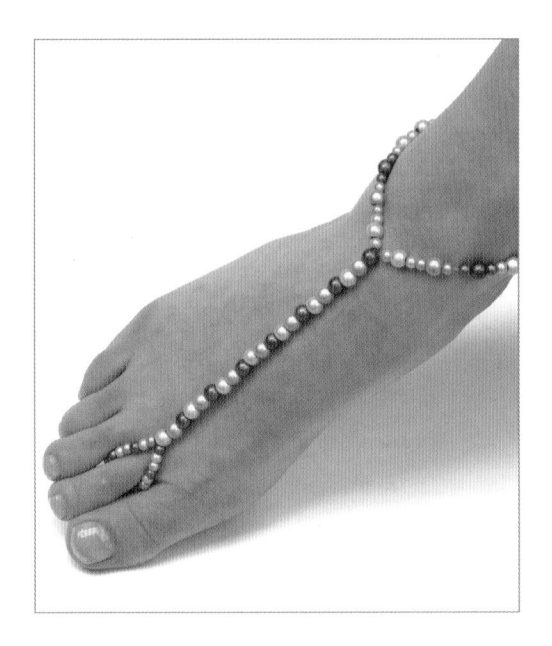

MATERIALS
+ *Plastic seed or pony beads*
+ *Elastic cord*

NOTIONS/TOOLS
+ *Measuring tape*
+ *Scissors*
+ *Glue, if required*

1 Take one measurement around your ankle and another measurement from your ankle to the base of the toe next to your big toe. To work out how much cord you need, take your ankle measurement, add two times the measurement from ankle to toe, and then add 3" (8 cm) more for the length of your toe and tying the knot.

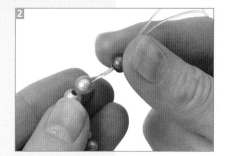

2 Thread on enough beads to go around your toe, bring these to the center of your cord, bring the two ends of the cord together and then begin threading on enough beads to go from your toe up to your ankle. Make sure these new beads go over both lengths of the cord.

3 Once you've threaded on enough beads to reach your ankle, separate the two cord ends and thread enough beads onto each one to reach halfway around your ankle. Bring the two cords together and knot the ends to secure.

4 To wear, put the large loop around your ankle and the smaller loop around your second toe.

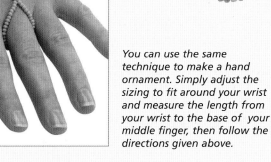

You can use the same technique to make a hand ornament. Simply adjust the sizing to fit around your wrist and measure the length from your wrist to the base of your middle finger, then follow the directions given above.

SIZE OF BEADS
You may want to use smaller beads to go around and under your toe or finger. These will be much more comfortable and less likely to cause irritation.

SAFETY-PIN CUFF

Use the humble safety pin (well, lots of them!) to great effect to produce

this funky cuff. Lots of bead and craft suppliers now have colored safety pins

like the ones we've used here, but an ordinary steel pin works just as well.

As ever, it's *your* choice of beads that makes the project special.

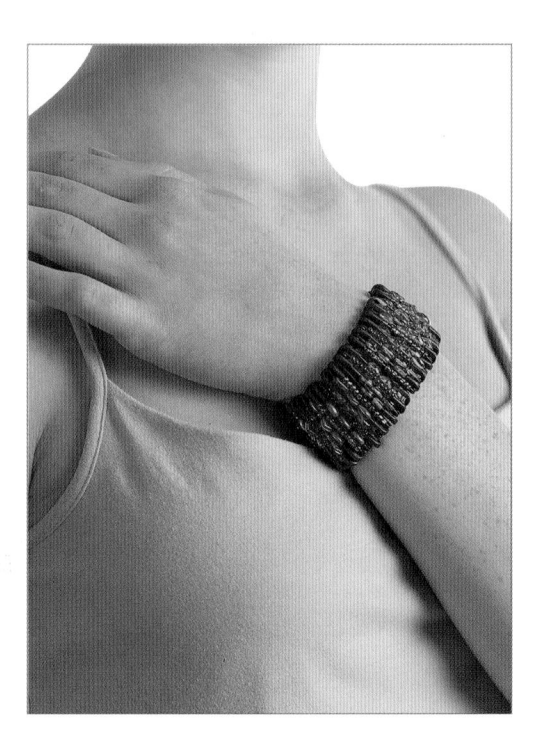

MATERIALS
✛ *Safety pins (see Step 1, below, to work out how many you will need)*
✛ *A selection of beads – they will need good-sized holes to thread onto the pins*
✛ *2 lengths of Stretch Magic elastic, each the circumference of your wrist plus 4" (9 cm)*
✛ *Adhesive tape*

NOTIONS/TOOLS
✛ *Measuring tape*
✛ *Scissors*

1 Measure your wrist. Don't worry about your wrist being smaller than your hand – the elastic will stretch over it! Work out how many safety pins you need by multiplying your wrist measurement by 10 (for example, if your wrist measures 7" (18 cm), you will need 70 safety pins).

2 Open a safety pin and thread beads onto the pointed arm. Close the pin. Repeat for all your safety pins.

There couldn't be a simpler but more effective beading project than this. It's a great way to get started and inspire you to learn more about beading.

3 Tape one end of one piece of elastic to your work surface (it stops the pins falling off). Thread all the safety pins onto the elastic, alternating top and bottom ends.

4 Tie the ends of the elastic together using the overhand knot described on page 51. Place the knot so that the pins sit next to each other with no gaps. Trim the ends of the elastic as described on page 51.

5 Thread the other length of elastic through the opposite ends of the safety pins. Tie and trim as before.

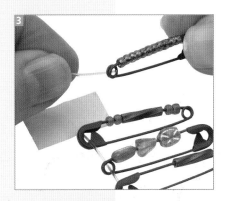

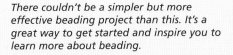

Cutting & filing wire

Some of the wirework techniques later in the book may seem a little complicated, especially if you are new to using wire. So start with this basic technique to give yourself a good grounding in the skills you will need later on. There are some basic tips that will help you when you are cutting or filing wire. Making sure that you are careful and accurate right from the start will help you to make a piece of jewelry you can be proud of.

CUTTING WIRE

Examine the wire cutters, as each make and model is slightly different and may give you a different result. Test your cutters on different thicknesses of wire and see whether holding them a certain way gives you a different result.

Generally, holding your cutters so that the flat side cuts the end of the wire will give you the best result. What you are looking for is a flat, smooth end.

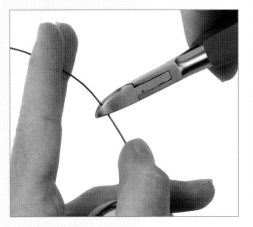

TAKE CARE

When using wire cutters you must make sure you don't cut yourself or injure yourself – or anyone else – with flying pieces of wire.

❖ Keep fingers and thumbs away from the cutting edge at all times.

❖ Point your work down and away from you – this reduces the chance of the wire flying upward. It is also a good idea to hold your finger over the piece of wire that is being cut away.

BAD TECHNIQUE

Using the slanted side of the blades to cut your wire will generally give you a point at the end – something you want to avoid.

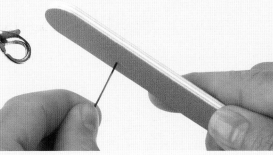

FILING WIRE

Once you have cut the piece of wire, you may need to file the end to remove any burrs that remain and to give a smoother finish that will sit nicely against the skin. You can use a specially designed metal file, sandpaper or even a nail file or emery board to get this result.

Making a simple loop on a head pin

Using wire with beads can be a really fast and effective way of making some stunning jewelry. A basic beaded unit can be as simple as one bead on a wire. Or you can thread on a lovely combination of beads. And beaded units can be combined in lots of different ways – so many choices!

Here we show you how to turn a loop on a head pin to make a basic bead and wire unit. We also tell you more about two of the tools we described earlier – wire cutters and round nose pliers.

Remember, you must be careful to use your wire cutters safely. See pages 58–9 for some cautionary words on cutting and filing wire correctly.

61

1 Thread a bead (or beads) onto a head pin or eye pin.

2 Holding the bead firmly against the bottom of the pin, bend the pin against the top of the bead at a 90 degree angle. Bend the wire using your fingers, or your snipe or flat nose pliers, if you prefer.

3 Supporting the pin against the bead from below, cut the wire so that between ¼–½" (1–1.5 cm) remains.

4 There are two ways of turning the loop. Choose one or the other – do not muddle them up.

A Hold the beads so that the cut wire is pointing away from you. Take the round nose pliers in your hand so that your thumb is on top and your other fingers are supporting the pliers from below. Rotate your arm away from you so that your thumb is now below and your fingers facing up to you. Grip the end of the wire with the tips of the pliers. Roll the pliers back toward you, bending the wire as you go. You may need to give an extra little turn to the loop to make sure there is no gap.

B Hold the beads so that the cut wire is pointing toward you. Bend your hand toward your body, then grip the wire and roll the wire away from you to form the loop.

5 Here is the completed loop.

BAD TECHNIQUE

These photographs show two incorrectly turned loops.

The top photograph shows what happens if you muddle up the two methods we have described in Step 4. If you turn the wire incorrectly, your loop would end up sitting next to the top bead (as shown here) instead of above it (as in step 5).

The bottom photograph shows what happens if you make a loop without bending the wire first (as described opposite in Step 2). It will give you a loop which is off to one side and not symmetrical.

BEADS WITH LARGE HOLES

You will sometimes want to use a bead that has such a large hole that the head pin slips through it. Do not despair – you can still use the bead, but thread a smaller bead on the pin first to hold it in place.

HEAD PIN EARRINGS

These crystal earrings are so simple to make using head pins. There are as many variations of this design as there are different beads – and you won't want to stop at one pair. Below, you'll find lots of variations to give you more ideas.

MATERIALS
+ 2 x 8 mm cube crystals
+ 2 x 6 mm cube crystals
+ 2 x 6 mm bi-cone crystals
+ 6 x 3 mm bi-cone crystals
+ 2 head pins
+ 2 earring wires

NOTIONS/TOOLS
+ Wire cutters
+ Snipe nose or flat nose pliers
+ Round nose pliers

1 Thread beads onto a head pin in the following sequence: 1 large cube, 1 x 3 mm bi-cone, 1 small cube, 1 x 3 mm bi-cone, 1 x 6 mm bi-cone and 1 x 3 mm bi-cone.

2 Bend the wire at a 90 degree angle at the top of the beads, cut off the excess wire.

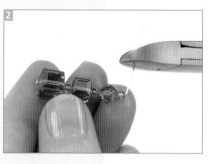

3 Turn a loop on the head pin (see pages 60–61).

4 Open the loop on an earring wire. Add the headpin and close the loop. Repeat from step 1 to make the second earring.

HERE ARE SOME IDEAS FOR YOU TO TRY

See how using different beads creates a different look? You can also build up a much more flamboyant earring by threading several head pins on the earring hook. If you are unsure about creating your own designs, look back to the advice given on pages 14–15 to help get you started.

BEAUTIFUL BROOCHES

We have used two types of safety pins for these projects. The first is a standard safety pin. In the second, the closure and pin sections can be separated. In both cases, these designs have the beaded units suspended from the fixed side of the safety pin so they are unaffected when the pin is opened and closed. Use the larger design as a brooch or to decorate a bag.

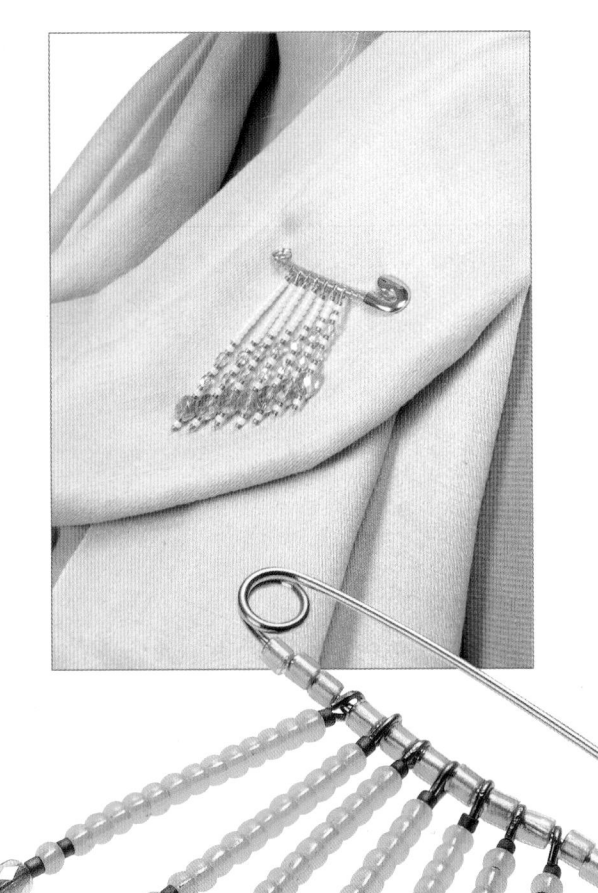

MATERIALS

Peach/turquoise brooch
+ *7 x 8 mm faceted beads*
+ *14 x 4 mm faceted beads*
+ *77 x size 11 seed beads (S)*
+ *63 cylinder beads (C)*
+ *12 x double size cylinder beads*
+ *2½" (6 cm) kilt pin with detachable closure*
+ *7 head pins ranging in size from 2½" to 1½" (6.5 cm to 4 cm)*

Blue/green brooch
+ *Approximately 30 mixed Czech glass beads*
+ *1½" (4 cm) safety pin*
+ *4 head pins of varying lengths*

NOTIONS/TOOLS
+ *Round nose pliers*

PEACH/TURQUOISE BROOCH

1 Thread the shortest head pin with beads in this sequence: 1C, 1S, 1C, 8 mm bead, 1C, 1S, 1C, 4 mm bead, 1C, 1S, 1C, 4mm bead, 1C, 1S, 1C, 1S, 1C. Make a loop at the top the head pin.

2 Thread the remaining head pins using the same sequence, but increasing the number of seed beads in the highest position by 2 beads each time. The final, longest, head pin will have 13 seed beads at the top. Detach the closure of the kilt pin.

3 Thread the beaded head pins on to the back of the kilt pin, spacing them out with the double cylinder beads. Screw the closure back onto the kilt pin.

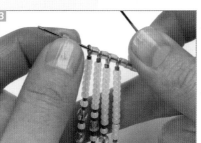

This "Fruit Salad' variation shows what happens when you fit as many head pins as possible onto a kilt pin.

BLUE/GREEN BROOCH

1 Thread roughly a quarter of the beads onto a head pin. Start to make a loop at the top of the head pin as described on page 61, but do not close the loop all the way. Slip the fixed back of the safety pin into the loop, then close the loop completely.

2 Thread beads onto three more head pins, varying the lengths slightly, and attach them to the safety pin as in step 1. Close the safety pin.

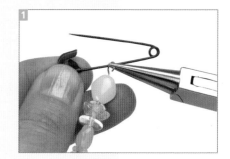

Making double-ended units & joining units together

Once you have learnt how to turn a single loop on a head pin, you can move on to making loops at both ends of your beads. These bead-and-wire units can then be joined together to make jewelry, either as you make them or, later, with jump rings.

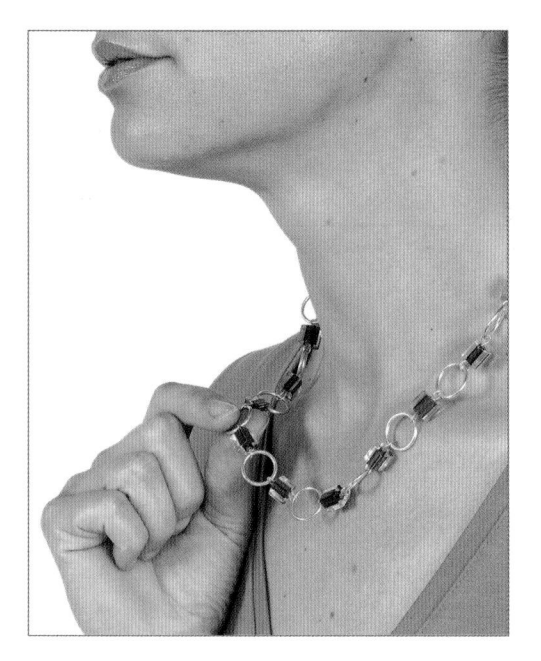

You can either cut the "head" off a head pin and use the straight piece of wire that remains, or you can buy craft wire on spools. These spools are available in many different colors and thicknesses, giving lots of opportunity for your creative imagination to run wild! Once you've mastered this technique the scope for variations is endless.

MAKING DOUBLE-ENDED UNITS

1 *Cut a length of wire 1½" (4 cm) longer than the bead you are using.*

2 *Grasp one end of the wire with round nose pliers and turn the pliers away from you to begin forming a loop. Continue making a loop until the wire touches itself. You may need to reposition the pliers to do this.*

3 *Once you have made the loop, insert one of the jaws of the round nose pliers into it and straighten it so that it sits centrally above the length of wire. You may need to adjust the loop if it opens slightly.*

4 *Thread a bead (or beads) onto the wire and, holding it firmly against the loop already made, bend the rest of the wire against the top of the bead at a 90 degree angle.*

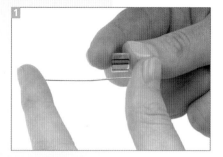

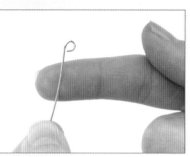

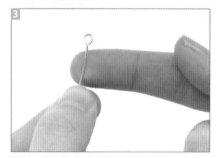

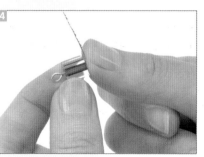

5 *Trim this wire so that between ¼–½" (1–1.5 cm) remains.*

6 *Using the round nose pliers, turn the second loop in the same way as you turned the first.*

JOINING UNITS

Open one of the loops using the technique described in "Opening & closing jump rings" on pages 26–7. If you find it hard to use two pairs of pliers you can hold the bead with one hand and use one pair of pliers to open the loop instead. Thread the open loop through a loop on another unit, and, reversing the method of opening the loop, close the loop to secure. You can also join them together using a jump ring.

SUMMER FLOWERS
NECKLACE

This summery necklace uses double-ended units that space the beads out, keeping the composition light (and making expensive beads go further). The dangles also drape well and can be longer than a single head pin.

MATERIALS

+ *1 x 15 mm square flower feature bead*
+ *3 x 12 mm square flower feature beads*
+ *5 x 10 mm square flower feature beads*
+ *30–50 x 6 mm round glass beads*
+ *30–50 x 4 mm faceted beads*
+ *Flexible beading wire*
+ *Clasp*
+ *Head pins*
+ *Crimps*

NOTIONS/TOOLS

+ *Wire cutters*
+ *Round nose pliers*
+ *Crimping, flat or snipe nose pliers*

1 To make the short dangles: thread a 10 mm feature bead onto a head pin. Make a simple loop (see page 60) on top of the bead. Cut the "head" off a head pin and use the wire to make a double-ended unit (see page 66) with a 4 mm faceted bead. Join the two units together (see page 67) Repeat for the second short dangle.

2 To make the medium dangles: thread a 12 mm feature bead onto a head pin and make a simple loop on top of the bead. Make a double-ended unit with a 10 mm feature bead and two more double-ended units with one 4 mm faceted bead on each of them. Join these units together, with the largest feature bead at the bottom, then a faceted bead, a feature bead and a faceted bead at the top. Repeat for the second medium dangle.

3 To make the longer dangle: thread the 15 mm feature bead onto a head pin and make a simple loop on top of the bead. Make a double-ended unit with a 12 mm feature bead and another with a 10 mm feature bead. Make three more double-ended units with one 4 mm faceted bead on each of them. Join these units together with the

largest flower bead at the bottom, then a faceted bead, the 12 mm flower bead, a faceted bead, the 10 mm flower bead and a faceted bead at the top.

4 Using the guidance under "Planning a design" on pages 14–15, decide how long you want the finished necklace to be and cut a length of flexible bead wire accordingly. Thread the wired components on to it, placing 3 beads (a faceted bead, a 6 mm round bead and a faceted bead) in between each component. Have the longest component in the center and the shortest at the sides. Add alternating faceted and 6 mm round beads evenly to each side of the central arrangment until you have the required length. Following the guidance on page 19, secure the clasp to each end of the wire with a crimp and trim off the excess wire.

This technique is not just for creating necklaces and bracelets. These earrings show how joining double-ended loops creates lots of swing in the dangles.

Making a wrapped loop on a head or eye pin

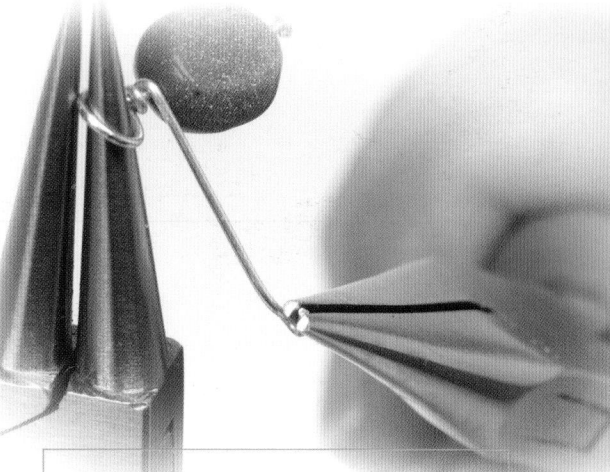

Making wrapped loops is a wirework technique which, although harder to do than simple turned loops, is well worth the effort.

Wrapped loops involve wrapping your piece of wire around itself, which is not only more secure than a simple turned loop, but also can be more decorative.

This technique can be complicated to learn – especially as you use two different types of pliers at one time – and you may not be happy with your loops at first. But with enough practice you'll soon be turning out professional wrapped loops.

However, unlike simple turned loops, once the loop is made it can no longer be opened. This means that you either have to use jump rings or findings that can open to attach your loops, or learn how to join them before they're finished, see page 75 for details.

WASTING WIRE

When making wrapped loops there will always be some wire wasted, this cannot be helped. This excess wire helps you to make the loop and is cut off at the end. Always make sure you take this into account when starting your loop, don't scrimp on the wire as it will only make your life harder.

LENGTH OF WIRE

The length of wire left at the top of the bead – between the bead and before the bend – is the area that will be covered by your wire wraps. So if you want less wraps make sure to leave less wire.

WRAPPING A LOOP

1 Thread your bead onto a head or eye pin, making sure you have at least 1" (4 cm) of wire left at the top of the bead. Using your flat or snipe nose pliers, hold the wire above the bead and bend the wire over at a right angle.

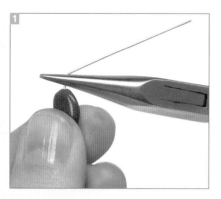

2 Grasp the wire at the bend with your round nose pliers, and then bend the length of wire around your pliers to form a loop. You can do this by pushing the wire with your fingers, or by holding the end of the wire with your flat nose pliers and pulling it around. You may have to loosen your round nose pliers and adjust their position as you do this to finish the loop. Bring the wire right around until it crosses over itself.

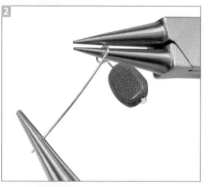

3 Hold the round nose pliers in your non-dominant hand with the points facing upward and the loop you have made placed over one of the jaws.

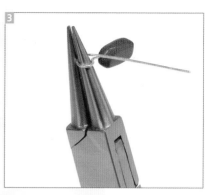

4 Now grip the end of your wire with your flat or snipe nose pliers and begin to wrap it around the small section of wire that sits above the bead, before the loop. The best way to do this is to "pull" the wire around in a large circle, going slowly to make sure the wraps sit neatly next to each other.

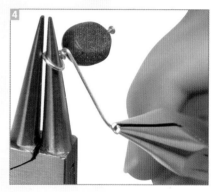

5 Continue wrapping until you have reached your bead, trim the wire and, using your flat or snipe nose pliers, push the cut end in so it doesn't stick out and catch. If you have a pair of crimping pliers you'll find them very useful here.

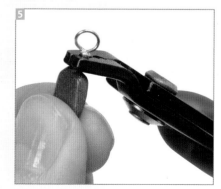

LOOP SIZE

The diameter of the place on the pliers where you wrap the wire will give you the size of loop you're going to make. So if you want a smaller loop, make sure you use the smaller end of your pliers.

NO GOING BACK

Once you start wrapping this loop it will be sealed shut and you won't be able to open it without cutting it off. Concentrate and make sure you're happy with this before you finish the loop.

DECORATIVE KEY-RING

Keep your keys secure and easy to find with this striking design that doubles as a decoration for your purse. We have used hollow metal beads because they are light and durable. To make the ring extra secure we have used the strength of the wrapped loop technique rather than a simple turned loop to complete each of the dangles.

MATERIALS

+ *3 round hollow metal beads,*
  ½" (1 cm) across
+ *4 bi-cone hollow metal beads*
  ¼" (0.5 cm) across
+ *4 disc hollow metal beads,*
  ½" (1 cm) across
+ *20 gold spacer beads*
+ *3 head pins, 2¾" (7 cm) long*
+ *2 split rings*
+ *1 key-ring, 1" (2.5 cm) across*
+ *1 attaching hook on chain*

NOTIONS/TOOLS

+ *Flat or snipe nose pliers*
+ *Round nose pliers*
+ *Wire cutters*

1 Take one head pin and begin to thread beads onto it in the following sequence: 1 round, 1 spacer, 1 round, 1 spacer, 1 round, 2 spacers.

2 Make a wrapped loop (see pages 70–71) on top of the final beads and trim off any excess wire.

3 Take another head pin and thread alternating bi-cone and spacer beads onto it, beginning and ending with a spacer bead. Make a wrapped loop on top of the last bead.

4 Take the final head pin and thread beads onto it in the following sequence: 1 spacer, 1 disc, 3 spacers, 1 disc, 3 spacers, 1 disc, 3 spacers, 1 disc, 1 spacer. Make a wrapped loop on top of the last bead.

5 Thread the three beaded head pins onto a split ring and thread it onto the key-ring. Thread the last link of the chain of the attaching hook onto a split ring and thread it onto the key-ring.

"Theme" a key-ring as a gift for a friend, or personalize it by spelling out her name using alphabet beads. You can also create fabulous key-rings using a mixture of inexpensive smaller beads and one or two special larger beads that really set the piece apart.

Double-ended wrapped loops

As already shown, wrapped loops are trickier to make but can be worth the effort. They can be joined together to make a chain or can be spaced out with jump rings. They can also be used to frame, highlight and space out expensive, more special beads, especially when you don't have enough beads to make a strung necklace.

Once you have wrapped your loop you will find it is impossible to open it again. This means that you have to join finished wrapped loops to each other with jump rings or other findings, or join them as you make them.

Note that with double-ended wrapped loops there will be twice the amount of wire on show, which might overpower smaller, more delicate beads. If this is the case you can reduce the number of wraps you make and thus the amount of wire on show.

MAKING DOUBLE-ENDED WRAPPED LOOPS

1 *Cut a length of wire at least 3"
(8 cm) longer than your bead. Place
your bead on the center of the
wire, and grasp the wire above the
bead with your flat or snipe nose
pliers. Keeping the pliers in that
position, remove the bead and
make your right angle bend.
Continue and form the wrapped
loop as normal and thread on the
bead.*

2 *Hold your bead firmly against the
wraps and, starting by making the
right angle bend in the wire, form a
wrapped loop at this end also.*

EQUAL WRAPS

*To ensure that your bead has equal amounts of
wraps at end each, make sure you use the same
pliers, and the same section on their jaws, each
time you hold the wire before making the bend. As
this is where your wraps will sit, differences in the
height of the wire will result in different amounts
of wraps.*

JOINING WRAPPED LOOPS

1 *Start by making your bend and loop
as normal. Then thread this loop
onto another wrapped loop or solid
jump ring etc.*

2 *Holding the loop as you normally
would, begin carefully wrapping
your wire around it.*

3 *Continue to form the wrapped loop
until finished.*

WHAT IF YOU FORGET TO JOIN THEM?

*If you forget to join the loops
together as you form them,
you can join them using jump
rings.*

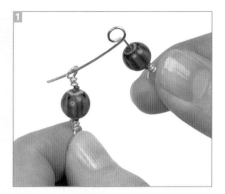

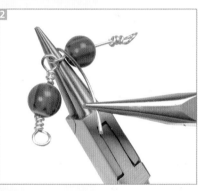

| PROJECT

BONE BEAD BRACELET

This bracelet is so easy to make but shows off a beautiful single bead perfectly. Choose a flattish bead that will sit comfortably on your wrist. Ours is a carved bone bead with a different design on each side, so it's really two bracelets in one.

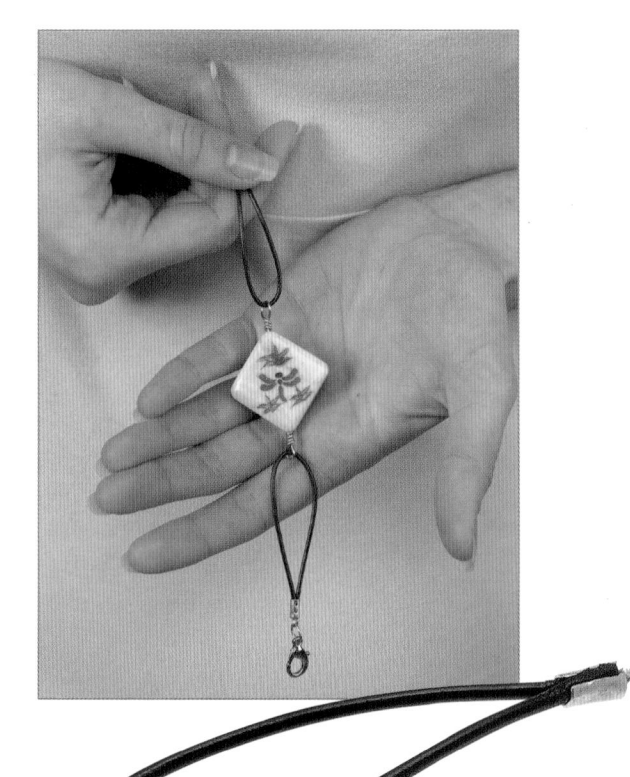

MATERIALS
÷ *1 large flat bead, approximately 1"*
  (3 cms) across
÷ *Fine leather thong (see Step 3, below, for lengths)*
÷ *1 lobster clasp*
÷ *2 jump rings*
÷ *2 cord crimps*
÷ *Wire*

NOTIONS/TOOLS
÷ *Scissors*
÷ *Measuring tape*
÷ *Wire cutters*
÷ *Flat or snipe nose pliers*
÷ *Round nose pliers*

1 Cut a length of wire approximately 3" (8 cm) longer than your bead. Make a wrapped loop (see page 71) at one end of it.

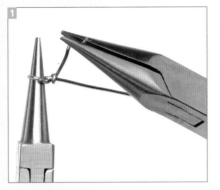

2 Thread the bead on the wire and let the bead drop down to the wrapped loop. Follow the directions given on page 75 to complete the second wrapped loop.

3 Attach each cord crimp to a jump ring. Attach one of the jump rings to the lobster clasp. Decide how long you want your bracelet to be. Lay the beaded unit against the tape measure at the center of this length and place one jump ring assembly at each end.

4 Measure the distance between the wrapped loop and the top of the cord crimp on one side of the bracelet. Cut a piece of leather thong twice that length, pass it through the wrapped loop and bring both ends together in the cord crimp. Close the crimp. Repeat this process for the other side of the bracelet.

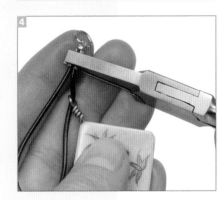

Whatever center bead you use, the simplicity of this technique brings out its beauty and the finished piece looks subtly stylish.

"FLOATING" NECKLACE & EARRINGS

The dyed mother-of-pearl beads used here are pretty and and light to wear. But, as with all drilled shells and semi-precious beads, their holes may be smaller than expected and you may need to use a finer wire than with some other beads. It is pretty much inevitable that you will find yourself wrapping the second loop of some units before threading them onto the necklace. Don't abandon them – use them to make earrings instead!

MATERIALS
+ *1 strand of mother of pearl 10 x 14 mm oval beads*
+ *0.7 mm/21-gauge silver wire*

NOTIONS/TOOLS
+ *Measuring tape*
+ *Wire cutters*
+ *Flat or snipe nose pliers*
+ *Round nose pliers*

1 Measure your bead.

2 Cut a length of wire 3" (8 cm) longer than the bead. Make a wrapped loop at one end (see pages 74–5). Thread a bead onto the wire, fitting it snugly up against the wraps.

3 Make a second wrapped loop to complete the first bead unit.

The large holes in these Peruvian ceramic beads meant we had to use much heavier wire in order to make sure that the beads were held in place by the wrapped loops.

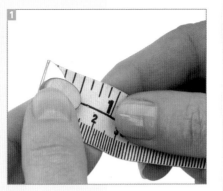

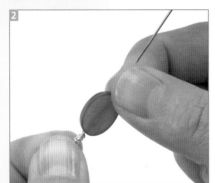

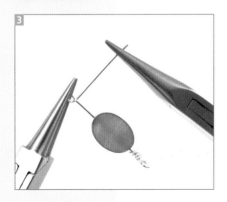

4 For the next unit, make the first wrapped loop as before and thread on your bead. Holding the bead firmly against the wraps with your flat or snipe nose pliers, bend the wire into a right angle and form a loop with your round nose pliers. It is IMPORTANT that you do NOT wrap the loop yet!

5 Take the first unit you made and thread it onto the wire of the new unit and maneuver it into the as yet unclosed loop. NOW you can wrap the loop and you will have successfully linked two double wrapped units.

6 Repeat steps 4 and 5 until you have the length you want, excluding the clasp. Thread one end of the necklace onto the S-hook clasp and your necklace is ready to wear.

EARRINGS

To make earrings to complete the look, make a double-ended wrapped unit. Open the loop of an earring hook, place one end of the unit into the loop and close it. Repeat.

| PROJECT

CHARM BRACELET

This charm bracelet is perfect for showing off those special beads you've bought or for bringing together a collection of different beads to make a finished piece. Using red lampwork beads on wrapped loops, we have used a hand-made jump ring chain but, you could buy a ready-made chain to decorate, or some charms to hang from your hand-made chain.

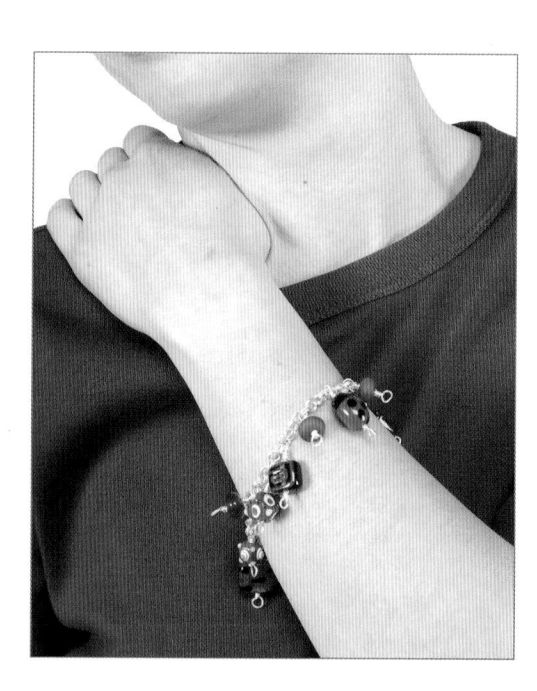

MATERIALS
+ *Approximately 100 jump rings or an existing chain bracelet*
+ *16–18 lampwork beads*
+ *1 clasp*
+ *0.8 mm/20-gauge silver wire*

NOTIONS/TOOLS
+ *Wire cutters*
+ *File or emery board*
+ *Flat or snipe nose pliers*
+ *Round nose pliers*

1 Making the chain If making your own chain, join the jump rings into a length long enough to circle your wrist comfortably. To make the chain stronger and more decorative, use two jump rings in each place instead of one. When you have the length required, attach a clasp to finish.

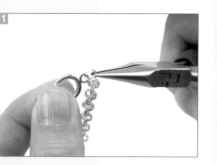

2 Decorating the chain Cut a length of wire 3" (8 cm) longer than your beads. File the ends to neaten, if required. Then turn a wrapped loop (see pages 70–71) at one end. Thread on your bead.

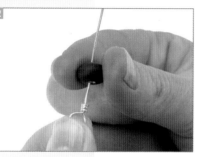

3 At the other end of the wire, make a second wrapped loop to finish the unit.

4 Continue making wrapped looped units with the rest of your beads.

5 Decide how you want your bracelet to look by laying your chain out with the beads beside it. Play with different combinations of beads before you begin to attach the beads to your bracelet.

6 Open one of the jump rings (see pages 26–7) on your chain and thread on your bead. Make sure you close the ring securely. Continue until you have added all your beads to decorate the chain.

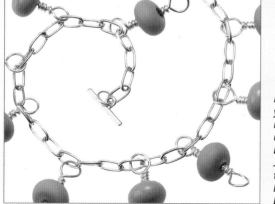

If you don't want to make your own chain, you can make a charm bracelet using a ready-made bracelet or bought chain. Just remember to loop the unfinished wrapped loop through the chain before you wrap it.

Using end cones

End cones are useful for hiding the connection between strands of beads and a clasp or other finding. This is particularly important when using multiple strands or dangles. Fixing the strands into the end cone with a wrapped loop ensures a strong and secure finish. In the instructions below, we have used an eye pin to make the wrapped loop. If you find you do not have any eye pins, just turn a simple loop onto a piece of wire instead.

1. Following the guidance on pages 14–19 on planning your design and using crimps, cut your first length of flexible wire and crimp as usual, but thread on an eye pin instead of a clasp. Thread beads to the length required, making sure you cover both ends of the wire.

2. Finish and crimp the second end of your flexible wire following the guidance on pages 18–19, using an eye pin instead of a clasp.

3. Make more strands, securing them onto the SAME two eye pins. The strands can be the same or different lengths, depending on your design.

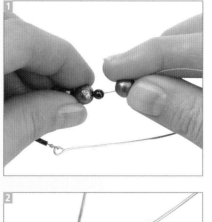

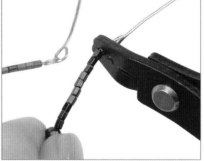

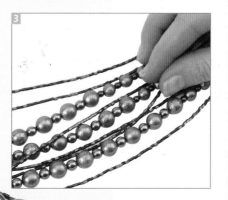

4. Thread one of the eye pins through an end cone from the inside. Hold the wire against the top of the end cone with your flat or snipe nose pliers. Bend the wire to 90 degrees against the pliers.

5. Make a loop with your round nose pliers. Wrap the loop with your flat or snipe nose pliers so that the wrapping is snug against the end cone and the strands are held firmly in place inside it. Trim the wire neatly.

6. Secure the other eye pin into a second end cone with a wrapped loop, as before. Attach your clasp or finding, using a jump ring if appropriate.

CHECK YOUR SIZES

The more strands you use, the larger your end cone needs to be. Also, you may need to use a larger eye pin to fit more than three or four strands onto one loop.

EARRINGS WITH END CONES & JUMP RINGS

You can really let your imagination run wild when making dangly earrings with end cones. You can vary the number of dangles, make some simple dangles and others that have "feature" beads. Just make sure you don't make them too heavy to wear.

NOTE ON MATERIALS

Before you start, check the sizes of your flexible beading wire and crimps. The wire should be fine enough so that four strands of it, rather than two, will go through a crimp. Make sure that the crimp you choose will hold the four strands firmly when closed.

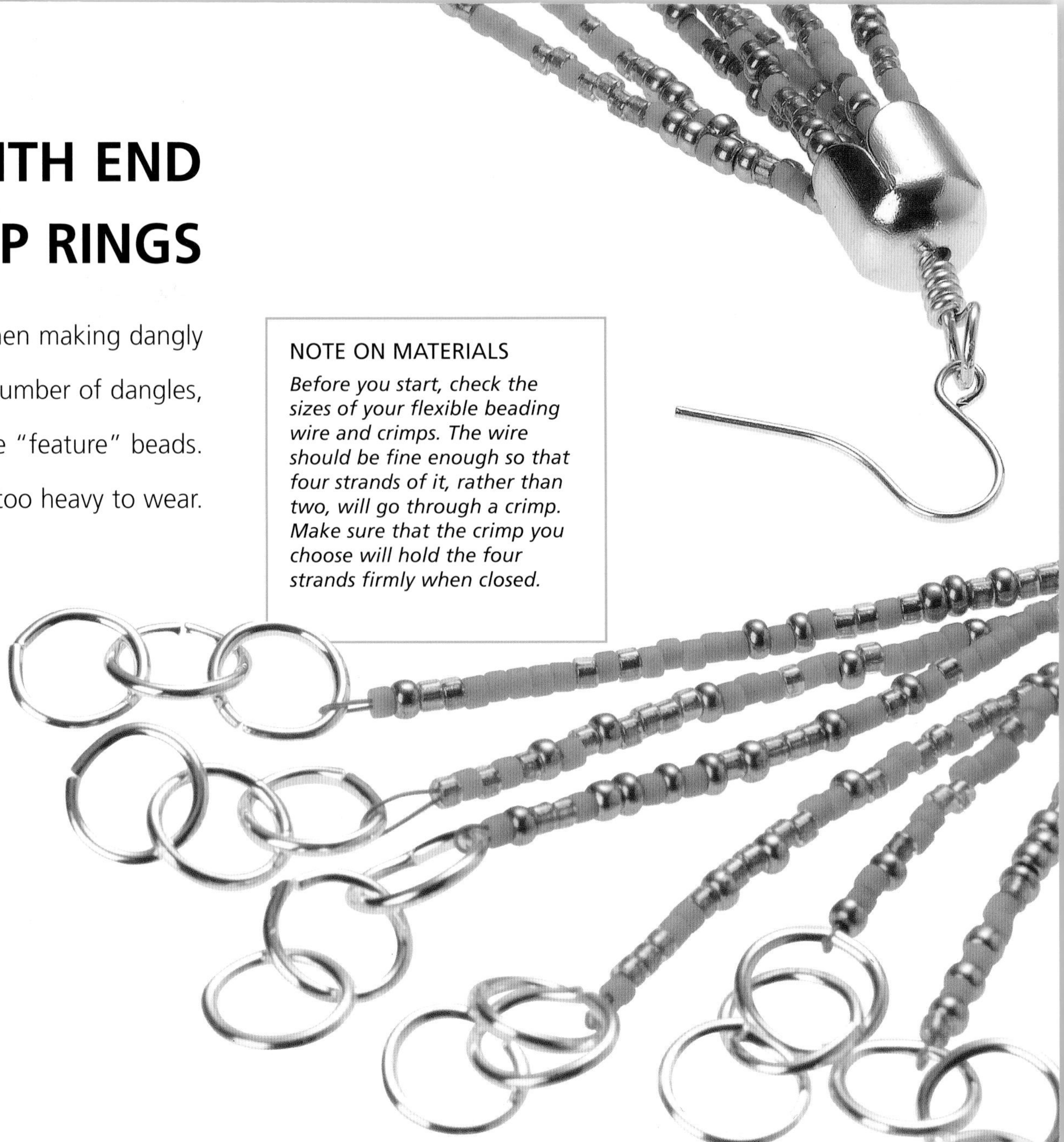

MATERIALS

÷ *A spool of flexible beading wire (fine)*
÷ *Seed beads and/or cylinder beads in three colors, mixed together*
÷ *Crimps*
÷ *12 small jump rings*
÷ *36 large jump rings*
÷ *2 end cones*
÷ *0.8 mm/20 gauge silver wire*
÷ *Earring findings*

NOTIONS/TOOLS

÷ *Wire cutters*
÷ *Flat or snipe nose pliers*
÷ *Round nose pliers*
÷ *Measuring tape*

1 Thread 1½" (4 cm) of beads onto a spool of flexible beading wire. Thread on a large jump ring and pass the wire back through all the beads.

2 Pull the wire through the beads so that there is 1½" (4 cm) of wire exposed above the beads and the wire is pulled tight onto the jump ring. Cut the wire from the spool 1½" (4 cm) away from the beads.

3 Thread a crimp and a small jump ring and take both ends of the wire back down through the crimp. Pull the wire up tight and close the crimp. Trim the wire close to the crimp.

4 Join two more large jump rings onto the jump ring at the bottom of the dangle to make a chain.

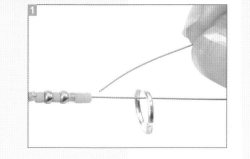

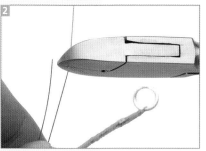

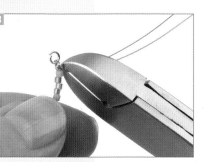

5 Thread 2" (5 cm) of beads onto the spool of flexible beading wire and repeat steps 1 and 2. Add a crimp and pass both ends of the wire through the same small jump ring already used. Pass the wires through the crimp and close it.

6 Trim the wire close to the crimp. Attach two more large jump rings at the bottom of the dangle as before. Now repeat as above until you have completed four pairs of dangles.

7 Cut a 4" (10 cm) length of silver wire. Using your round nose pliers, make a loop at one end of the wire. Open the loop and thread on the four jump rings. Close the loop.

8 Thread the wire through an end cone and secure with a wrapped loop as described on page 71. Attach the wrapped loop to an earring finding. Repeat the whole process for the second earring.

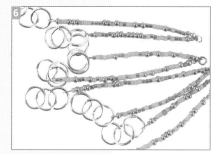

PROJECT **WRAPPED LOOPS BELT**

This great belt is easy to make and if you make it long enough it can be worn by anyone – or the same person in different ways.

Because it uses a simple hook fastening you can wear it any length you like, tight with a long tail or looser with a shorter tail.

MATERIALS
+ *A strand of large semi-precious beads. You could use chunks, flat ovals, round beads, or any shape that takes your fancy*
+ *10 mm jump rings. You will use 3 for every bead you use*
+ *8 mm/20-gauge wire in a metal to match your jump rings*
+ *S-hook clasp or other clasp with a hook on it*

NOTIONS/TOOLS
+ *Wire cutters*
+ *Crimping, flat or snipe nose pliers*
+ *Round nose pliers*

1 Cut a length of wire 3" (8 cm) longer than your bead. Use this wire to make a wrapped loop at either end of your bead (see pages 70–71). Continue until all of your beads have been wrapped.

You can use this technique to make many different styles of jewelry. This necklace uses heart-shaped faceted beads on wrapped loops, which are then joined together with two jump rings, one on top of the other.

2 Using your pliers, add a jump ring to one loop of your bead (see pages 26–7). Add another two jump rings, making a chain of three.

3 Add a wrapped bead to the third jump ring and repeat, adding beads separated by three jump rings until you have used up all of your wrapped beads.

4 Add your hook clasp to one end of your final wrapped-loop bead and secure it. When you wear your belt you can link this hook into any of the jump rings, so you can wear the belt at different lengths.

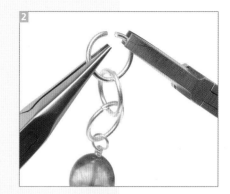

Making a clover-leaf shape

Once you've learnt some basic wire techniques, it's time to play around with your new knowledge and make some wire shapes. These simple shapes are easy to learn but may take some practice to get them neat and even. This is one occasion where you will really want to make sure you use the same spot on your round nose pliers to turn your loops, as you want them to look as even as possible. See page 61 for help on getting your loops the same size.

1. Cut a length of wire at least 3½" (9 cm) long.

2. Hold one end of the wire with your round nose pliers and turn the wire until it touches itself, making a "P" shape.

3. Hold the wire just below the first loop and turn a second loop to convert the "P" into a "B". You may find this easier if you push the wire around the pliers with your thumb or finger.

4. Make a third loop to the side of the lower loop.

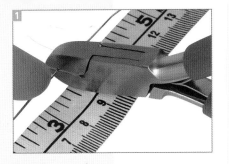

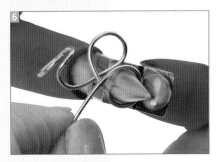

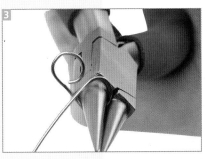

5. Bend the first loop down so that you can grasp the wire next to the third loop.

6. Turn the fourth loop so that the wire points in toward the center of the clover-leaf shape.

7. Push the first loop back up into place.

8. Trim the long length of wire in the center of the shape so that it does not overlap any other wire. If you need to, you can tighten or adjust any of the loops using your round nose pliers.

BIGGER SHAPES

Why not go bigger? You can always form the loops around larger round objects, such as a pen or bead tube to make bigger and bolder shapes.

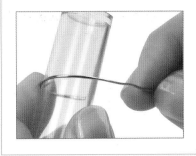

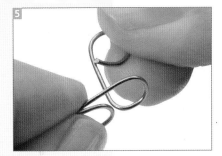

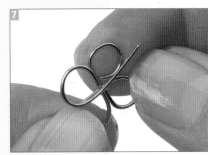

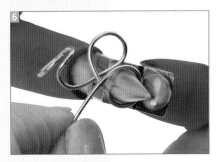

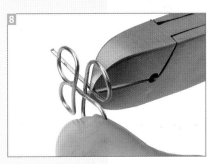

THREE-LEAF CLOVER EARRINGS

Simplicity is the watchword with these eyecatching earrings. The addition of a single crystal bead makes them very special, lightweight, and easy to wear. This project gives you a great opportunity to practice making clover leaf shapes, which can be tricky at first.

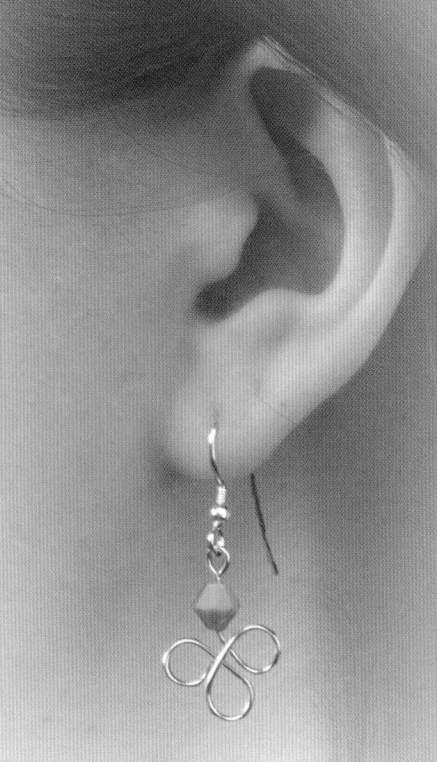

MATERIALS
+ *0.8 mm/20 gauge silver wire*
+ *2 x 5 mm crystals*
+ *Pair of earring findings*

NOTIONS/TOOLS
+ *Wire cutters*
+ *Flat or snipe nose pliers*
+ *Round nose pliers*
+ *Measuring tape*

1 Using your wire cutters and measuring tape, measure and cut two lengths of wire 3" (7.5 cm) long.

2 Using your round nose pliers and following the guidance given on pages 88–9, begin turning a clover leaf shape. Stop once you have turned three leaves.

3 Using your flat or snipe nose pliers, hold the long length of wire just after the third leaf and bend it slightly, so that the wire points straight up between the first and third leaf.

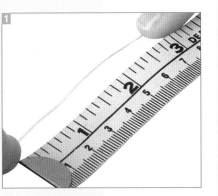

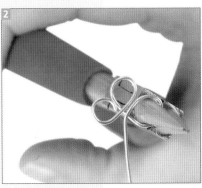

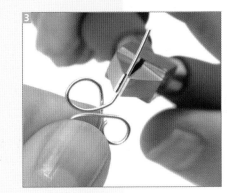

4 Thread a crystal onto the wire and add a turned loop to the end.

5 Open the loop on one of your earring findings and thread on your clover leaf. Close the earring finding. Repeat all of the above steps to make a second earring.

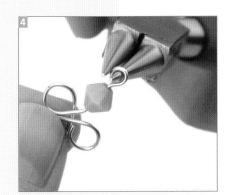

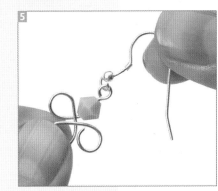

You can achieve so many looks with this technique. Whether you use one-off beads or more everyday varieties, you'll have the pleasure of knowing that your clover leaves are all your own work!

FLOWER BROOCH

Stack two clover-leaf shapes on top of each other to create this pretty brooch. We used brightly colored wire to give a flowery effect. The back of the brooch has been covered with dark sequins and beads so that the metal is hidden and the flower stands out well. For this project, instead of using pliers, we made the clover-leaf shapes by wrapping the wire around two different-sized bead tubes. Experiment a little to get the sizes you want – you can use any round shape.

MATERIALS
+ 0.8 mm/20 gauge colored craft wire
+ Flat sequins, ¼" (0.5 cm) across
+ Size 11 seed beads
+ 3 x size 8 seed beads
+ Metal brooch back with sieve 1⅛" (3 cm) across
+ Flexible beading wire
+ Crimps

NOTIONS/TOOLS
+ Wire cutters
+ Flat or snipe nose pliers
+ Empty bead tube, 2¼" (6 cm) around
+ Empty bead tube, 2" (5 cm) around
+ Measuring tape

1 Cut a 12" (30 cm) length of wire from your spool of craft wire. Wrap the wire around the larger of your two forms to make a clover leaf shape, following the instructions on pages 88–9. Repeat with the smaller form, using a 10" (25 cm) length of wire. Set both wire shapes to one side.

2 Cut a 20" (50 cm) length of flexible wire. Place a crimp at one end of the wire and close it. Thread the other end of the wire through a hole on the outside edge of the sieve of the brooch back (from the rear). Thread on a sequin and a tiny seed bead. Put the end of the wire back through the sequin and through the same hole in the sieve.

3 Pull tight to secure the sequin and bring the end of the wire up through the next visible hole on the edge of the sieve. Repeat until you have added sequins all round the edge of the sieve. Then, moving toward the center, bring the wire up through the nearest visible hole.

4 Add sequins to the surface of the sieve, working around in a circle just inside the first circle. Bring the wire up through the hole in the center of the sieve.

5 Thread on a sequin and let it drop down to the sieve. Lay the larger clover-leaf shape over the sequin with the wire coming through one of the loops of the shape. Take the wire across the center of the shape and down through the opposite loop, the sequin and the center hole of the sieve. Pull the wire all the way through so that the clover shape is held firmly in place.

6 Thread on a tiny bead and bring the wire back through both the center hole and sequin again. Lay the smaller clover-leaf shape over the first so that all eight loops show. Thread on three size 8 seed beads and stitch the smaller leaf shape in place, through the sequin and the center hole of the sieve.

7 Thread on a crimp and let it fall to the back of the sieve. Squash the crimp closed over the wire as close as possible to the sieve and trim the wire close to the crimp.

8 Place the sieve over the back of the brooch, making sure that all four "clamps" are exposed. Press each clamp down with your snipe nose pliers, taking care not to catch in the sequins around the edge.

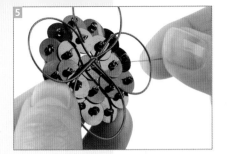

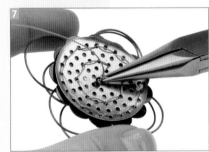

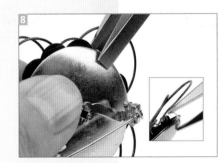

CLOVER-LEAF BRACELET WITH WRAPPED LOOPS

These pretty clover leaves are just the thing to separate beads on wrapped loops. Highly decorative and subtly sophisticated, while this bracelet is a little more complicated to make, your patience will be rewarded time and again. Use different colored wires to match your beads and experiment with different size loops.

MATERIALS
+ 0.8 mm/20 gauge gold wire
+ 4 glass beads, approximately ¼"
  0.5 cm across
+ Clasp

NOTIONS/TOOLS
+ Wire cutters
+ Round nose pliers
+ Flat or snipe nose pliers
+ Measuring tape

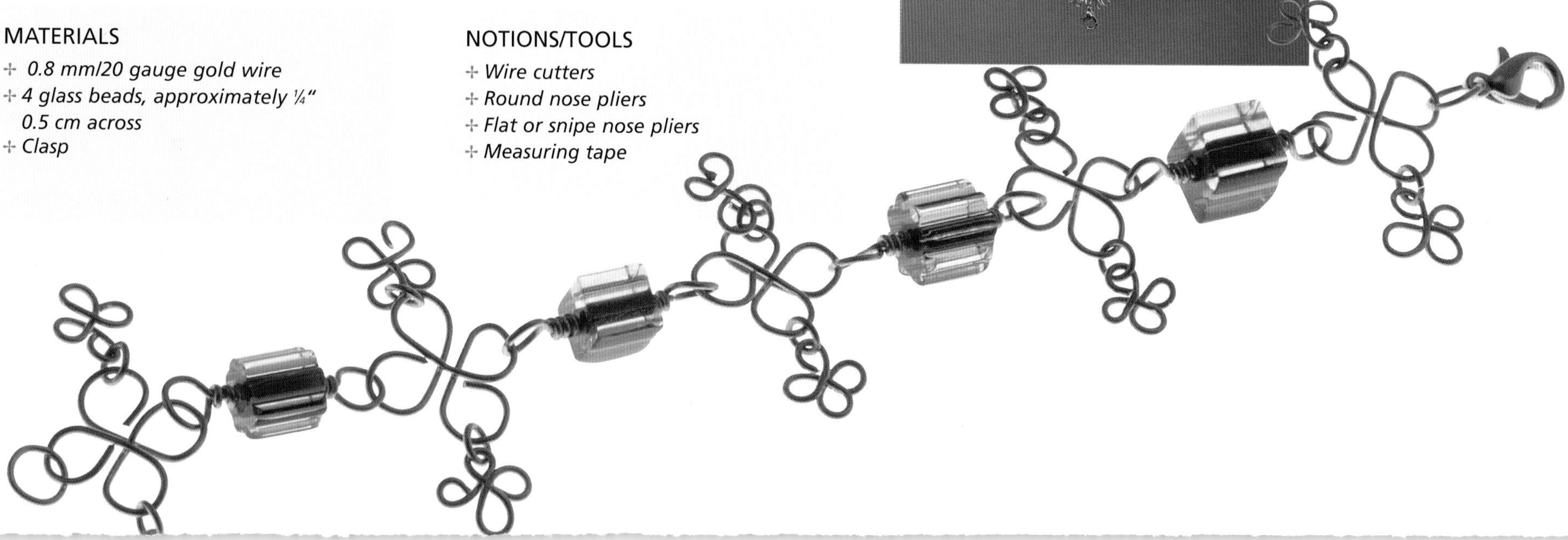

1 Following the instructions on pages 88–9, form five clover-leaf shapes.

2 Cut a length of wire 3" (8 cm) longer than your bead. Following the instructions for making wrapped loops on pages 70–71, form a loop at one end of the wire and thread on a clover-leaf shape.

3 Wrap the loop and thread on a bead.

IF YOU FORGET

As you make the wrapped loops, remember to thread on your clover-leaf shapes.
If you do forget to thread one on before wrapping a loop, all is not lost. Carefully open the first or last loop of the clover-leaf shape, as you would a jump ring. Thread on the wrapped loop and close down the leaf shape again.

1

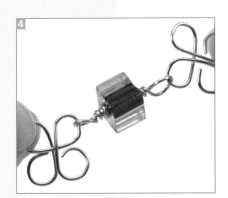

2

3

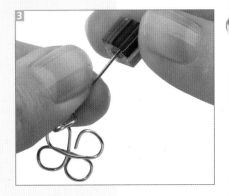

4 Make a loop the other side of the bead, leaving a gap to allow for wrapping. Thread on a clover leaf and wrap the loop.

5 Repeat from step 2, building up a chain of alternating clover-leaf shapes and wrapped loop units. Make 2 smaller clover-leaf shapes for each large shape. Attach one to each side of the larger shapes with a jump ring.

6 Add a clasp, extending it with jump rings if necessary for the length you require.

4

5

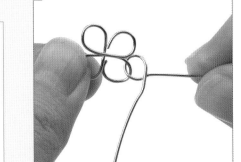

6